BARRON'S SIMPLIFIED APPROACH

TO THOREAU'S

Walden

By Robert L. Gale

ENGLISH DEPARTMENT
UNIVERSITY OF PITTSBURGH

BARRON'S EDUCATIONAL SERIES, INC.

WOODBURY, NEW YORK

CHRONOLOGY

	Thoreau	Other Writers	American History
817	Born July 12 in Concord, Massachusetts	Bryant, "Thanatopsis"	Seminole Indian and Negro uprising in Florida
818			Andrew Jackson fights in first Seminole War
819		Irving, "The Sketch Book"	
820			Missouri Compromise (Maine admitted as free state 1820, Missouri as slave state 1821)
821		Cooper, "The Spy"	
823	Moves with family from Chelmsford and Boston back to Concord	Cooper, "The Pioneers," "The Pilot"	Monroe Doctrine
824			Oregon Trail opened as trade route
826		Cooper, "The Last of the Mohicans"	Lyceum program begun in Millbury, Massachusetts
827	Writes "The Seasons," his first extant essay	Poe, "Tamerlane and Other Poems"	
828		Webster, "An American Dictionary of the English Language"	Construction begun on Baltimore and Ohio Railroad
829		Poe, "Al Aaraaf, Tamerlane, and Minor Poems"	Andrew Jackson inaugurated president (1829-37)
831		Poe, "Poems"	
832		Bryant, "Poems"; Irving, "The Alhambra"	

v

	Thoreau	**Other Writers**	**American History**
1833	Enters Harvard College		
1835	Emerson settles in Concord		Abolitionist tracts burned in Charleston South Carolina
1836		Emerson, "Nature"; Holmes, "Poems"	Battle of the Alamo (Texas independence recognized 1837; Texas admitted to Union 1845)
1837	Graduates from Harvard; teaches briefly in Concord school	Emerson, "The American Scholar"; Hawthorne, "Twice-Told Tales"	Financial panic (followed by depression lasting until 1843)
1838	Opens short-lived school in Concord with his brother John (closed 1841); begins to lecture for Concord Lyceum; begins to read widely in Oriental literature	Emerson, "Divinity School Address"; Whittier, "Ballads and Anti-Slavery Poems"	Maine-New Brunswick territorial disputes (settled 1842 underground railroad established to transport runaway slaves
1839	Conducts excursion in September with his brother John resulting in "A Week on the Concord and Merrimack Rivers"; falls in love briefly with Ellen Sewall		
1840	Begins publishing essays and poems in "Dial" magazine	Dana, "Two Years Before the Mast"; Poe, "Tales of the Grotesque and Arabesque"	
1841	Begins to live in Emerson's house as handyman	Emerson, "Essays"	Brook Farm experiment begins (lasts until 1847)
1842	John, Thoreau's brother, dies of lockjaw	Longfellow, "Ballads and Other Poems"	
1843	Publishes translation of "Prometheus	Poe, "Prose Tales"	

Thoreau	Other Writers	American History
Bound" by Aeschylus in "Dial"; goes briefly to Staten Island as tutor for children of Emerson's brother William; meets Horace Greeley in New York		
1844 Makes pencils; accidentally sets Concord woods on fire while cooking fish with a friend	Emerson, "Essays, Second Series"; Lowell, "Poems"; Whittier, "Voices of Freedom"	
1845 On July 4 begins to live at Walden Pond	Poe, "The Raven and Other Poems," "Tales"	
1846 Goes to jail for one July night for refusing to pay poll-tax; travels to Maine in September	Hawthorne, "Mosses from an Old Manse"; Melville, "Typee"	Mexican War declared in May
1847 Leaves Walden Pond September 6; again lives in Emerson's house	Emerson, "Poems"; Melville, "Omoo"	Mexican War ends in September
1848	Lowell, "Biglow Papers," "A Fable for Critics," "Poems: Second Series"	Peace treaty after Mexican War ratified in May
1849 Publishes "A Week on the Concord and Merrimack Rivers" and "Civil Disobedience" in May; visits Cape Cod in October	Melville, "Mardi," "Redburn"; Parkman, "The California and Oregon Trail"; Holmes, "Poems"	California gold rush begins
1850 Revisits Cape Cod in June; goes to Long Island in July to seek Margaret Fuller's drowned body	Emerson, "Representative Men"; Hawthorne, "The Scarlet Letter"; Melville, "White-Jacket"; Whittier, "Songs of Labor"	Compromise of 1850 (California to be admitted as free state, states to be organized out of other Mexico-ceded territory without restriction as to slavery, fugitive slaves to be

	Thoreau	Other Writers	American Histor‹
			returned more effi-ciently, etc.)
1851	Health worsens	Hawthorne, "The House of the Seven Gables"; Melville, "Moby Dick"	
1852		Hawthorne, "The Blithedale Romance"; "The Poetical Works of Oliver Wendell Holmes"; Melville, "Pierre"; Stowe, "Uncle Tom's Cabin"	
1853	Visits Maine in September		
1854	Gives "Slavery in Massachusetts" speech at Framingham on July 4, publishes "Walden" in August		Commodore Matth‹ C. Perry opens Jap to American trade; Kansas-Nebraska ‹ (permits squatter sovereignty in Kans and Nebraska, lea to violence in Kans in 1855 and 1856)
1855	Sick in the spring; visits Cape Cod in July; in fall receives magnificent library of Oriental literature from British disciple and sends Whitman's "Leaves of Grass" and other American books in return	Longfellow, "The Song of Hiawatha"; Whitman, "Leaves of Grass"	
1856	Does surveying in New Jersey for rural experimental community in fall; meets Whitman in Brooklyn	Emerson, "English Traits"; Melville, "Piazza Tales"; Whitman, "Leaves of Grass" (second edition)	
1857	Meets John Brown in February; visits Cape		Dred Scott decisior (against Scott; test‹

Thoreau	Other Writers	American History
Cod in June and Maine in July-August		constitutionality of Missouri Compromise and opined that Negroes were not American citizens); financial panic
1858	Holmes, "The Autocrat of the Breakfast-Table"; Longfellow, "The Courtship of Miles Standish"	Lincoln-Douglas Debates; Republican Party gains strength
1859 Thoreau's father dies; reads "A Plea for John Brown" in October in Concord		John Brown raids Harper's Ferry, Virginia, in October; is hanged in December
1860 Camps in August with Channing on Monadnock; publishes "The Last Days of John Brown"; reads and publishes "The Succession of Forest Trees"	Emerson, "The Conduct of Life"; Hawthorne, "The Marble Faun"; Holmes, "Elsie Venner"; Whittier, "Home Ballads and Poems"	
1861 Goes to Minnesota in vain effort to improve his health	Whitman, "Leaves of Grass" (third edition)	Civil War begins in April
1862 Dies May 6 of tuberculosis in Concord	Howe, "Battle Hymn of the Republic"	
1864 "The Maine Woods"		
1865 "Cape Cod"; "Letters to Various Persons"		
1866 "A Yankee in Canada"		
1894 "Familiar Letters"		
1906 "Journals" (14 volumes); "Walden Edition" (20 volumes)		
1943 "Collected Poems of Henry Thoreau"		
1958 "The Correspondence of Henry David Thoreau"		

THOREAU'S LIFE

Henry David Thoreau, 1817-62, was the only one of the many New England writers associated with Concord, Massachusetts, who was born there. Later, for the benefit of those who wondered if he had traveled extensively, he wrote, "I have traveled a good deal in Concord." This characteristic comment shows his loyalty to the place of his birth and also his irrepressible fondness for punning, for wherever he went in nature, there was harmony.

Thoreau's forebears were French, Scotch, and English. His name, pronounced in his time as THAW-roe or perhaps THUR-roe, came from a French-speaking Isle of Guernsey ancestor. Thoreau's father, John, who had inherited a good deal of property from his successful Boston father but had lost it in unlucky business experiments, was a pencil maker during the future writer's youth. Thoreau sporadically helped out at this chore of pencil-making. His mother Cynthia was intelligent, energetic, nature-loving, and according to some a bit domineering. Thoreau had an older sister Helen, a beloved brother John (also older), and later a younger sister Sophia. His brother's death by lockjaw in 1842 was one of the most profound sorrows of Thoreau's life. Helen, a teacher who died of tuberculosis in 1849, helped pay Thoreau's way through Harvard College. Sophia survived her brother, whom she devotedly nursed during his fatal sickness; later she helped defend and augment his reputation.

Thoreau was a normal boy in a typically busy family. Early in life, however, he demonstrated an unusual love of nature and of language, by writing an essay entitled "The Seasons" when he was only ten years old. Perhaps his exceptional mental alertness helped the family decide to send him to college in spite of his older brother John's never going on with any advanced schooling. At any rate, Thoreau went to the Concord Academy and then in 1833 entered Harvard, where during this period there was a group of young men destined to distinguish themselves in many ways: Richard Henry Dana, Jr., back from California and the sea, both of which he wrote about in *Two Years Before the Mast,* joined Thoreau's class of 1837; James Russell Lowell, the future poet, critic, professor, and diplomat, was in the class of '38; so was William Wetmore Story, the future law scholar, expatriate sculptor, and writer; and there were several others. It used to be thought that Thoreau was shy, introverted, scholastically mediocre, and reclusive at Harvard. But the facts are that he was convivial enough, gay humored, and devoted to reading whatever engaged his powerful mind. During his junior year, he suffered a serious sickness, which understandably forced him into a lower scholastic position than he would otherwise have occupied. During this same academic year Thoreau met Orestes Brownson, an aggressive and initially liberal New England clergyman, who acted as a catalyst to speed the process of his intellectual maturing.

Upon graduation Thoreau became a teacher in the Concord school system. But within a few weeks the school committeemen tried to tell him how to discipline his charges; so he ferruled half a dozen pupils chosen at random—to show his disgust with the system—and then resigned.

The following summer he set up a progressive private school of his own in a Concord house, where he was soon joined by his kindly brother John. Moving into the Concord Academy building, they soon had all the students they could desire. The curriculum and discipline were enlightened: the classics, mathematics, sports, nature study, a little surveying, but no flogging. Unfortunately, early in 1841 John Thoreau's health showed signs of breaking, and the thriving school had to be closed.

Thoreau was not sorry to quit teaching, since his heart had never been in it and it did not challenge his essential self. Evidently Miss Ellen Sewall, however, did to a degree. From Scituate, southeast of Boston, this young lady had come to visit Concord in the summer of 1839, and both Thoreau and his brother seem to have fallen in love with her. The following summer John visited her on the coast, proposed, was accepted, and then was rejected. Apparently knowing nothing about all this, Thoreau himself proposed by letter in the fall. Miss Sewall's ministerial father considered the whole Thoreau family too liberal and therefore forced the girl to decline again. It is possible that her refusal relieved the already philosophical young Thoreau.

Infinitely worse than losing Miss Sewall was Thoreau's loss of his brother, who in January, 1842, cut his finger while stropping a razor; tetanus developed, and in ten days he was dead. Thoreau later penned a moving poem called "Brother Where Dost Thou Dwell?", which reads in part:

> Is thy brow clear again
>   As in thy youthful years?
> And was that ugly pain
>   The summit of thy fears?

> .   .   .   .

> Dost thou still haunt the brink
>   Of yonder river's tide?
> And may I ever think
>   That thou art at my side?

A substitute brother was Ralph Waldo Emerson, who shortly after his move to Concord in 1835 must have begun to inspire Thoreau, fourteen years his junior but like him observant, nature-loving, poetic, and Transcendental. By the time Thoreau returned from Harvard in 1837, he probably already knew well the eminent author of *Nature* and "The American Scholar." The two men had their minor differences later on, for neither was very sociable and neither wanted anyone to sway him from his own natural orbit. So the commonly repeated statement that "Thoreau practiced what Emerson preached" is obviously unfair. Even more damaging were Lowell's unkind poetic lines concerning Thoreau, from *A Fable for Critics*:

> There comes ———, for instance; to see him's
>   rare sport,
> Tread in Emerson's track with legs painfully
>   short;
> How he jumps, how he strains, and gets red in
>   the face,
> To keep step with the mystagogue's natural
>   pace!
> He follows as close as a stick to a rocket
> His fingers exploring his prophet's each pocket.
> Fie, for shame, brother bard! with good fruit
>   of your own,
> Can't you let neighbor Emerson's orchards
>   alone?

But the truth is that Thoreau always respected Emerson and his second wife Lidian, lived in the Emerson house as a handyman in 1841 and again in 1847-48 when the sage revisited Europe for about seven months, and was to be memorably eulogized by Emerson at his death. In addition, Emerson al-

ways encouraged his writing and enlisted his aid in editing the
Dial magazine, the Transcendental organ from 1840 to its
demise in 1844; and in 1843 he dispatched Thoreau to Staten
Island to be tutor to his brother William Emerson's children,
on condition that the young writer have much leisure to compose and get into New York to seek publication of his early
efforts.

But Thoreau was happy and productive only in the Concord area. Home again, he soon renewed his habit of exploring
woods and ponds, fields and rivers, often accompanied by William Ellery Channing. This young man was the nephew of
the redoubtable Unitarian minister to whom Emerson ad-
dressed his famous "Channing Ode," and the brother-in-law
of the curious female Transcendentalist Margaret Fuller.
Young Channing may have given Thoreau some impetus toward his Walden Pond experiment by deserting Harvard and
living for a short time in a hut on the Illinois prairies. And
Channing wrote the first of many distinguished biographies of
his revered friend Thoreau.

Happy in the woods, Thoreau must have been deeply
hurt when he and a young friend from Harvard, while cooking their catch of fish in April, 1844, let some sparks get away
from them. The resulting fire consumed a hundred acres of
Concord woods, and for years afterwards Thoreau was reviled
by many unsympathetic townspeople as the shiftless fellow
who had destroyed the valuable property of others.

The same cruel April witnessed the collapse of the *Dial*,
to which by this time Thoreau had sent more than thirty contributions. Since he had been unable to make any literary con-
tacts in New York and the *Dial* was now defunct in Salem,
Thoreau must have begun to feel unwanted and at the same
time to cast about to see how he could direct his pulsing
thoughts into a new channel. Before long he had decided to

build a cabin beside Walden Pond and live there in comfortable solitude. Channing may have had a good deal to do with his immediate decision, for early in 1845 he wrote Thoreau: "I see nothing for you in this earth but that field which I once christened 'Briars'; go out upon that, build yourself a hut, & there begin the grand process of devouring yourself alive. I see no alternative, no other hope for you. Eat yourself up; you will eat nobody else, nor anything else."

In the fall of 1844 Emerson had bought about fourteen acres by the shore of Walden Pond, less than two miles south of Concord. Late the following March Thoreau borrowed an axe, began clearing a two-acre field of its briars, and then started building his immortal shack. On the Fourth of July he took up his residence in it, to begin the experiment of simplifying his life.

Thoreau explains unforgettably in "Where I Lived, and What I Lived For," which is Chapter Two of *Walden,* exactly why he went out to the pond. "I went to the woods because I wished to live deliberately, to front only the essential facts of life, and see if I could not learn what it had to teach, and not, when I came to die, discover that I had not lived. I did not wish to live what was not life, living is so dear . . ." Dearest to him in life were simple manual labor, boating, hiking, communing with nature, reading, writing, and pondering essentials. In "Visitors," Chapter Six of *Walden,* Thoreau makes it clear that he did not live utterly alone and aloof out at the pond. He often tramped back to Concord, and almost as often people came out to scrutinize their unusual neighbor and his residence.

When he chanced to visit Concord in July, 1846, he was taken into custody by his friend Sam Staples the constable and jailed overnight for refusing to pay his poll-tax. Thoreau had been refusing for some years, unwilling to support a government which tolerated slavery and, more recently, had instigated the Mexican War. In his stirring essay "Civil Disobedience," which was the literary result of his brief imprisonment, he wrote in part, "I did not for a moment feel confined, and the walls seemed a great waste of stone and mortar. I felt as if I alone of all my townsmen had paid my tax. . . . I could not but smile to see how industriously they locked the door on my meditations, which followed them out again without let or hindrance, and *they* were really all that was dangerous." The following morning Thoreau was free again because someone, probably an aunt, paid his tax, to his outrage. There is a story, perhaps apocryphal but certainly illuminating, that when Emerson sauntered down to interview the prisoner and asked, "Why are you here?", Thoreau came back with a brilliant rejoinder: "Why are you not here?"

The next month Thoreau wandered even farther away from Walden Pond than the town jail when he journeyed into the wilds of Mount Katahdin, the highest point in rugged Maine. He reveled in the natural scenery there and vowed to return if he could. "What a place to live," he later wrote, "what a place to die and be buried in! There certainly men would live forever, and laugh at death and the grave." Soon he was back in the Concord area, which now meant for him simply the pond.

It is likely that Thoreau did not go to Walden to gain the raw materials for his book *Walden* but instead to find the time to write *A Week on the Concord and Merrimack Rivers,* his *ave atque vale* to his brother John, who had shared the boating excursion on the two rivers back in 1839. And he wrote other works at Walden as well, including a splendid essay on Thomas Carlyle. Soon enough, however, he must have seen that the experimental life he was leading at that moment was worthy of being memorialized in a book. By February, 1847, he was lecturing in Concord on his experiences beside the pond, and some of the phrasing of those lectures found its way into his book *Walden*.

In the spring of 1847 he greatly pleased a group of Harvard scientists, including the recently arrived Louis Agassiz, by sending them specimens of fish, snakes, and turtles whose habitat was Walden Pond. He even invited Agassiz to join him in a spearing expedition, but the professor was too busy writing lectures and supervising his laboratory students. In 1850 Thoreau was made a member of the Boston Society of Natural History; but three years later when nominated to the Association for the Advancement of Science, he declined membership because he felt that his scientific vision was colored by his Transcendentalism. And so the scientist Agassiz and the philosopher Thoreau failed to get together.

His metaphysical experiment in simplifying his life had succeeded at Walden beyond his dreams, and so on September 6, 1847, Thoreau was ready to begin a different phase. He explained his reasons for leaving Walden clearly enough: "I left the woods for as good a reason as I went there. Perhaps it seemed to me that I had several more lives to live, and could not spare any more time for that one." Within a month he was back in his old room in the home of Emerson, who was soon to leave his family to go on an extensive lecture tour through England and Scotland. Thoreau wrote a celebrated letter to his former mentor pretending that it was hard for the Walden veteran to adjust to his new assignment: "It is a little like joining a community, this life, to such a hermit as I am; and as I don't keep the accounts, I don't know whether the experiment will succeed or fail finally." With the innocence of one utterly pure in thought and deed, he then reported: "Lidian [Mrs. Emerson] and I make very good housekeepers. She is a dear sister to me." And he added of Emerson's little son Eddy, "He very seriously asked me, the other day, 'Mr. Thoreau, will you be my father?' . . . So you must come back soon, or you will be superseded."

When Emerson returned from England in July, 1848, Thoreau went back to his father's home, made innumerable pencils with him, did more surveying and writing, and chafed at the delays and rejections of publishers whom neither he nor Emerson could interest in *A Week*. Finally a Boston publisher agreed to print it if Thoreau would pay the $500 in expenses involved, and the book came out in May, 1849. In its back pages the imminent publication of *Walden* was advertised, but *A Week* sold so badly that *Walden* languished for five years. *A Week* was unfavorably reviewed, and by 1853 only 219 copies of the one thousand-copy edition were sold. The copies which remained, less some seventy-five which had been given away, the publisher finally sent to the philosophical author, who noted in his journal, "I have now a library of nearly nine hundred volumes, over seven hundred of which I wrote myself. Is it not well that the author should behold the fruits of his labor?" And Lowell accused Thoreau of lacking a sense of humor! On the more somber side, Thoreau was obliged to manufacture a thousand dollars worth of pencils and pencil materials and then sell them at a loss to clear his debt to the publisher.

Between the publication of *A Week* and that of *Walden,* Thoreau remained busy and sweet-tempered. Off and on he prepared graphite, did surveying, lectured, and of course kept on writing. In October, 1849, he explored Cape Cod with his friend Channing. In July, 1850, he went to Long Island, at the request of several Concord citizens, to try to recover the body of Margaret Fuller, who had drowned with her Italian husband Angelo Ossoli and their child during a storm off Fire Island on their return from Rome. Her body was never found,

nor was the manuscript of her history of the Roman revolt
of 1848-49. In September, Thoreau and Channing took a train
to Canada and explored Montreal and Quebec on foot. In
October, 1851, Thoreau helped a runaway slave from Virginia
escape from Concord a step ahead of the authorities, and make
his way to freedom in Canada. The year 1852 must have been
especially memorable for Thoreau, because he remained close
to Concord and recorded 750 pages of personal observations
in his journal during the slowly changing seasons. In September of the following year he revisited the Maine woods, this
time in the company of an especially fine Indian guide, who
helped to awaken in him a desire to write a book about Indian
lore, a book destined never to be. Late in 1853 Thoreau got
in touch with Ticknor and Fields, Boston publishers, and
early the next year they told him that they would soon issue
Walden.

Thoreau's journal for August 9, 1854, reads as follows:
"To Boston. *Walden* published. Elder-berries. Waxwork yel-
lowing." Success came more rapidly for *Walden* than for *A
Week*. It was only seven years before the first printing of 2,000
copies was sold out. But disciples appeared more quickly.
Daniel Ricketson, a Quaker from New Bedford, wrote three
days after the publication of *Walden* to praise the author for
his humanity, cultivation, philosophy, originality, and poetic
style. Thomas Cholmondeley journeyed from England in the
fall to visit Emerson, but, meeting Thoreau at the same time,
he soon neglected the older writer for the younger one, to
whom he sent forty-four carefully chosen Oriental books from
London the next year. Thoreau was ecstatically pleased and
built shelves of Concord River driftwood for them. He expressed his gratitude for the "princely gift" in a letter and by
sending several American volumes, including Whitman's
Leaves of Grass, to Cholmondeley, who at the time was off

to the Crimean War half a world away. By the time he revisited Concord in 1858, Thoreau had many more admirers
and followers. Some of them, like Horace Greeley, Harrison
G. O. Blake, and Franklin Benjamin Sanborn, had been dev-
otees of long standing and revered Thoreau only the more
after the publication of his masterpiece.

Thoreau's last eight years following *Walden* were marked
by sickness, lecturing, surveying, some little traveling—often
on foot—mounting interest in abolition, and utterly imper-
turbable spirits. Early in 1855 a mysteriously debilitating mal-
ady left him with a lingering weakness in his formerly tireless
legs. The same spring he started publishing chapters of his
Cape Cod in *Putnam's Monthly Magazine* but soon differed
with its censorious editor—as he later did with Lowell of the
Atlantic Monthly over a passage in his *Maine Woods*—and
so he withdrew his material before the last installments could
be printed. The following winter he grew a Quaker-looking
beard to protect his sensitive throat from the biting cold. In
the spring of 1856 Greeley offered him the position of tutor to
his children; however, much though Thoreau liked and was
indebted to Greeley, he declined. In the fall he visited Bronson Alcott and other friends in New Hampshire and Vermont,
but the mountain and river-bank hiking he indulged in con-
vinced him quickly that he was not regaining his former physical resilience. Still, in November he went to an abolitionist's
farm-and-school community called Eagleswood near Perth
Amboy, New Jersey, to survey its two hundred acres and lecture to its young people. More important, at this time Thoreau
met Walt Whitman in Brooklyn, through their mutual friend
Alcott. As Thoreau wrote a friend in December, "Walt
Whitman . . . is the most interesting fact to me at present. I
have just read his 2nd edition [of *Leaves of Grass*] (which he
gave me) and it has done me more good than any reading

for a long time. . . . Since I have seen him, I find that I am
not disturbed by any brag or egoism in his book. He may turn
out the least of a braggart of all, having a better right to be
confident. He is a great fellow."

In February, 1857, Sanborn brought Captain John Brown
to Thoreau's house. The fated leader of the anti-slavery forces
in bleeding Kansas made a deep impression, but Thoreau was
no joiner and therefore remained aloof. His comment, "I wonder men can be so frivolous almost as to attend to the gross
form of Negro slavery, there are so many keen and subtle
masters who subject us both," echoes Emerson's better-known
one about having "quite other slaves to free than those Negroes, to wit, imprisoned spirits, imprisoned thoughts." But
two years later, when John Brown returned to the Concord
Town Hall to lecture and then quietly slipped away to raid
Harper's Ferry, Virginia, disastrously, Thoreau knew that he
had been in the presence of a memorable hero willing to die
for justice above the law. On October 30, 1859, five weeks
before Brown's execution, Thoreau summoned his townspeople
and delivered the first oration in America to defend and praise
"weird John Brown, the meteor of the war," as Herman Melville called him in "The Portent."

In 1860 Thoreau was the head of the family pencil-making
business, since his father had died early the previous year. This
responsibility, as well as his own worsening health, interfered
with his literary plans, his lecturing, and his walking tours.
Still, in August he and Channing took their last hike together,
camping on Monadnock Mountain in New Hampshire. In
October, Greeley printed in his New York *Tribune* the brilliant lecture on "The Succession of Forest Trees" which Thoreau had delivered to a nearby agricultural society and which
is his most important purely scientific work. In December
while counting rings in some tree stumps, Thoreau lay in the

snow and caught a severe cold, which his insistence upon meeting a lecture commitment soon after only made worse.

The following March he was still sick. In fact, he was still an invalid in May when, depressed also because of the Civil War, which had just started, he accepted the companionship of Horace Mann's son and traveled via Niagara Falls and Chicago to Minnesota. Thoreau observed the scenery, the wild life, and many Sioux Indians there, but he knew now that he was dying. So he returned to Concord in July, hoping to put his many fragmentary essays into better shape before the end. In this task and in other ways his sister Sophia devotedly helped him. Ironically, early in his last year Ticknor and Fields informed him that they wanted to publish a second edition of *Walden* and also to buy up the unbound sheets of his *Week* and issue it again. He loved to have little children visit him, and only regretted that more did not come by to chat. To one well-meaning adult who queried him on his readiness for the next world, he said simply, "One world at a time." When an aunt wondered whether he had made his peace with God, he said reassuringly. "I did not know that we had ever quarreled." On May 6, 1862, he leaned back on his pillow and, murmuring "moose" and "Indian," died very easily.

In his eulogy of Thoreau, his friend Emerson spoke of an inaccessible flower "called . . . by the Swiss *Edelweisse,* which signifies *Noble Purity*. Thoreau seemed to me [Emerson went on] living in the hope to gather this plant, which belonged to him of right. . . . The country knows not yet, or in the least part, how great a son it has lost. . . . His soul was made for the noblest society; . . . wherever there is knowledge, wherever there is virtue, wherever there is beauty, he will find a home."

In addition Emerson said that Thoreau "had exhausted

the capabilities of this world," which is of course not true.
Thoreau planned a book on Indian lore, a history of Concord,
and a "Kalendar" describing natural phenomena through all
phases of all the seasons. He also wanted to visit the West
Indies and the Far West. If he had been granted time to do
so and had then carried to completion his various literary proj-
ects, his admittedly great fame might be still more inspiring.

WALDEN

1. Economy

Thoreau begins by explaining that he wrote most of *Walden* while he was living for two years and two months at Walden Pond a mile from any neighbor and in a house which he had built himself. He wryly apologizes for talking so much about himself, by saying that he knows himself best and further that many acquaintances have asked him detailed questions about his mode of life at Walden. (1-2*)

Then Thoreau launches into a statement of his belief that the lives of many people are full of misfortune which could be avoided if they would only be less materialistic. Coarse labor only makes people insensitive to the finer things of life; then they attach more importance to material necessities and luxurious extensions thereof, which puts them into debt and makes them even more deadened to spiritual values. It becomes ridiculous, therefore, to prate about Negro slavery, when the mass of men are desperately enslaved themselves. Truly, "The mass of men lead lives of quiet desperation" (9). (3-9)

Thoreau then adjures his readers to give up their prejudices, refuse to be lectured by their elders, and dare instead to live more simply and with more self-reliance. (10-15)

If we consider the source of our troubles, we will soon see that it lies in the fact that we have made foolish luxuries into necessities. To some creatures, for example the bison, the only necessity is food (plus a little water). No brute needs more

---

* In this summary of *Walden*, references are not to pages but to paragraphs.

15

than food and shelter. For man in the Concord climate, food, shelter, clothing, and fuel are the only necessities; and it is possible that long ago the over-use of fire for warmth made that former luxury a present necessity. Essentially, the function of necessities is to keep the vital heat in us. Thoreau then reports that, so far as he is concerned, he needs only the simple necessities and in addition a few implements, such as an axe and a wheelbarrow, and lamplight, stationery, and access to a few books. The so-called comforts of life are actually hindrances, because their pursuit prevents men from "adventur-[ing] on life now" (20). Next Thoreau makes it clear that he is prescribing not to those who are happily employed but to those who complain inconsolably that they are sacrificing themselves to what they call duty. (16-21)

Now Thoreau begins to explain his desire in life. He has wanted under all circumstances to improve his time. Prefacing his next remarks with the comment that the reader must "pardon some obscurities," he then says, "I long ago lost a hound, a bay horse, and a turtle-dove, and am still on their trail" (24). Seeking them, he has long desired not merely the dawn but nature herself, to listen for a message in the wind, to be a "reporter to a journal, of no very wide circulation [namely, his own diary]" (28), to be an inspector of storms, and to be herdsman of "the wild stock of the town" (29)—in short, to mind his own business. He is reminded of the Indian basket-weaver whose wares a well-to-do Concord lawyer refused to purchase, to the dismay of the starving Indian. Thoreau too has woven "a kind of basket of a delicate texture" (31); however, he feels no necessity to sell his creations. Knowing that his fellow-citizens will not be likely to offer him "any curacy or living" (32), he has turned to the woods, planning while he is there to think like a tradesman, exporting certain native products, seeing to details, being his own telegraph, exploring, studying, and in short making of Walden Pond "a good place for business" (34). (22-34)

His business decided upon, Thoreau next catalogues those items which are indispensable for his job. Clothing is first. We should pay less attention to new clothes, let all clothes age, avoid occupations which require new clothes, resist whims of fashion and in fact laugh at all fashions rather than merely the ones which happen to differ from our own, and be critical of mass-produced clothing. (35-41)

Another necessity of modern life is shelter. We should imitate the Laplander and the Indian by insisting upon a simple house. Recall that men's first houses were hollow or shelving rocks and caves. Today an adequate house can be constructed of wooden boxes no bigger than railroad-line toolsheds. Houses are so expensive now that fewer human beings than animals own adequate shelter, for which reason the majority of people rent their shelter from a minority of well-to-do landlords. The savage owns his wigwam because it is cheap, whereas the civilized man usually rents his abode because he can afford no other course. The average house today requires too much "life . . . to be exchanged for it, immediately or in the long run" (45). If it is said that the poor will always be with us, perhaps it is time that the old proverb is destroyed. Thoreau reports that he has ascertained that while most Concord farmers have toiled for decades, not a dozen own their land. It is not the farmer who gains the land but the land which gets him. However, suppose that the majority are able to own their homes and that they are improvements over the savages' dwelling places; have modern men progressed morally also? We must still consider our poor minority, silently living in shanties and sties and shrinking with cold and misery. (42-53)

Not only our houses should be simple and inexpensive,

but our furniture as well. Thoreau recalls becoming so discontent when some pieces of limestone on his desk became dust-catchers that he threw them out the window. Railroad cars are so expensively appointed that safety and convenience are neglected, and men have become so encumbered with accessories that they "have become the tools of their tools" (56). In the seventeenth century, our ancestors survived by burrowing into the American earth for their first shelters; only later did they beautify their homes. Also remember: "let our houses first be lined with beauty . . . and not overlaid with it!" (58). Further, we should avail ourselves of modern construction materials such as boards, shingles, lime, and bricks. (54-59)

And now Thoreau begins to describe his experiment in fashioning a simple house in the woods. In March, 1845, he borrowed an axe—later returning it well sharpened—and with spring in the air but with a little ice still on the pond, began felling "some tall, arrowy white pines, still in their youth, for timber." Once, while swelling a new axe-handle in a pond-hole, he saw a torpid snake there and compared its sluggish state to that of many low and primitive human beings "waiting for the sun to thaw them" (60). On April 1, rains melted the last of the ice. Thoreau went on cutting timber, making studs, rafters, and 6″ by 6″ beams, often only partly hewn, mortising and tenoning, and relishing his dinner of bread when held in his pitchy hands. By mid-April his house was framed. For boards and nails he purchased a railroading Irishman's shanty for $4.25. In a hill-side Thoreau dug his cellar 6′ by 6′ and 7′ deep, noting that since even splendid houses have cellars more permanent than the houses, "The house is still but a sort of porch at the entrance of a burrow" (65). Early in May he and some neighborly neighbors raised his house-frame. On July 4 he took possession. As soon as his roof-boards were feather-edged and lapped against the rain, he laid a foundation for his

chimney, which, however, he built of pond-stone only after
his fall hoeing and before a fire was necessary indoors. Meanwhile he did his "cooking . . . out of doors on the ground,
early in the morning." He was too busy to read much at this
time, but the few scraps of papers he chanced to come by
"afforded [him] as much entertainment, in fact answered the
same purpose as the Iliad" (66). (60-66)

We ought to build our own houses, as do the birds, which
sing at nesting. Our houses ought to have functional ornamen-
tation only; the first strong wind will strip off decorations if
they are hollow. (67-68)

Before winter, Thoreau reports, he built his chimney and
shingled his sides. So he then had a shingled and plastered
house, 10' by 15' by 8', with a garret and a closet, a window
on each side, two trap-doors, a door at one end and a brick
fireplace at the other, and a woodshed adjoining. He is proud
to itemize its cost and total it at $28.12½. Next he favorably
compares the cost of his house with the annual rent a college
student pays for poorer quarters; in addition, while the young
scholar only studies life, Thoreau "earnestly *live*[*s*] it from
beginning to end" (73). This rebuking of colleges leads Thoreau to criticize other "modern improvements" (74): we build
a telegraph line from Maine to Texas, perhaps only to find
that Maine and Texas have nothing to communicate to each
other; we build railroads but have to work longer to pay the
fare to Fitchburg than it takes Thoreau to walk there; and we
forget that while passengers ride the railroads, the railroads
run over their million Irish laborers. Thoreau wishes that his
laboring brethren "could have spent [their] time better than
digging in this dirt" (76). (69-76)

Now Thoreau presents a financial report. Before he finished his house, he planted 2½ acres with beans and some
potatoes, corn, peas, and turnips. His income from this crop

was $8.71½ after expenses. The second year he did better and still without hiring any animals for help; feeling that the average keeper of stock is herded by his herd, he did not "commit so great a blunder as to use the labor of animals" (79). This recollection inspires Thoreau to digress on the subject of laboriously produced towers and pyramids and tombs. Then, returning to his statistics he adds that he earned $13.34 in town at odd jobs—surveying, carpentry, and day-labor. From July 4 to March 1 he consumed $8.74 worth of food and would blush to report it but for the fact that the food bills of most of his readers would look worse in print. In all, his expenses—house, farm, food, clothing, oil, etc.—came to $61.99¾. His income in all was $36.78. Therefore his net living expenses were $25.21¾, which was nearly the amount of cash with which he started his experiment. His food cost him about 27¢ a week. Thoreau next takes delight in describing the simplicity of his diet—rice, purslane from his own cornfield, unleavened hoe-cakes of Indian meal and salt, and molasses made of pumpkins and beets. (77-88)

Then Thoreau turns to the subject of his home-made furniture, which he prized above the more costly things of many a mortgaged man. Well-furnished people are often properly likened to butterflies caught in spiders' webs. Thoreau had no curtains, never objecting to the sun and moon looking in on him. He advises us to imitate the savages, who cast their slough annually by means of a ritualistic fire into which they throw the sweepings of their houses; the Mexicans, he adds, used to practice a similar purification every fifty-two years. (89-96)

As for labor, Thoreau says that he can earn enough by working about six weeks a year to support himself for the rest of the year. This procedure freed his winters and most of his summers for study. He tried school teaching, he explains, but gave it up because he had to dress too well and also because he taught only for his livelihood and not for the good of his fellow-men. He then considered becoming a professional huckleberry picker. But he concludes that "trade curses everything it handles" (97). To those who appear to love work for its own sake he can say nothing; as for himself, he can earn his way through life by pursuing pastimes, since his needs are simple. He does not want people to imitate him but instead hopes that "there may be as many different persons in the world as possible" and that each person will "pursue *his own way,* and not his father's or his mother's or his neighbor's instead" (100). Others might wish to share dwellings or at least a common wall, but for himself Thoreau prefers a solitary house to any cooperation with others. (97-101)

Finally, he answers the charge that his conduct is unphilanthropic by stating frankly that doing good does not agree with his constitution, further that the do-gooders' profession is full, that goodness tainted is hideous, and that it is difficult to tell precisely what gifts the poor need most. Thoreau would prefer striking at the root of evils instead of spending time and money to alleviate misery only temporarily. Perhaps the best help one can offer is to inspire in others a sense of courage and goodness instead of inveighing that the whole world is miserable. The best praise of God is "a simple and irrepressible satisfaction with the gift of life" (110). (102-110)

Thoreau closes by summarizing a passage from Sadi, who says that the only tree which does not produce fruit and then consequently go through a dry season is the cypress, which the Persians call *azad,* meaning "free." Thoreau quotes the moral: "if thy hand has plenty, be liberal as the date tree, but if it affords nothing to give away, be an azad, or free man, like the cypress." Not being laboriously fruitful, Thoreau will be free and ever vernal. (111)

NOTES*

3 ** Sandwich Islanders—Hawaiians. Bramins—high-caste Hindus, who often penitentially torture themselves to demonstrate their indifference to things physical.

3-4 Hercules, Iolas, Augean stables—one of the twelve labors of Hercules, classical strong-man, was to kill the nine-headed Hydra, which Hercules's servant Iolas helped him to kill; another labor was to clean King Augeas's stable of 3,000 oxen, which he scrubbed out by diverting a river through it.

5 Deucalion and Pyrrha—the only two people on earth spared by the Greek god Zeus when he once became enraged; a divine voice suggested that they throw their mother's bones behind them, and when they did so the bones became human beings who endured (see Ovid, *Metamorphoses,* I). Sir Walter Raleigh, 1552?-1618—Elizabethan soldier, poet, and historian.

8 William Wilberforce, 1759-1833—British parliamentarian who urged the abolition of slavery in the British West Indies.

12 John Evelyn, 1620-1706—British man of letters who wrote among many other works *Silva, or a Discourse on*

---

* For help when I was compiling these notes to *Walden,* I am grateful to several previous editors of Thoreau, especially Francis H. Allen, ed., *Walden* (Boston: Houghton Mifflin Co., 1910); Bartholow V. Crawford, ed., *Henry David Thoreau* (New York: American Book Company, 1934); Joseph Jones, *Index to Walden: with Notes, Map, and Vocabulary Lists* (Austin, Texas: Hemphill's, 1955); David Gordon Rohman, "An Annotated Edition of Henry David Thoreau's *Walden,*" unpubl. diss. (Syracuse, 1960); and Walter Harding, ed., *The Variorum Walden* (New York: Twayne Publishers, Inc., 1962).

** References are to paragraphs.

Forest Trees, 1664 (from which the quotation is taken), and *A Philosophical Discourse of Earth,* 1676 (later called *The Compleat Gardener*).

15 Confucius, c. 550-478 B.C.—Chinese philosopher, *Analects,* II, compiled by his disciples.

17 Charles Darwin, 1809-82—English naturalist, who voyaged off South America, including Tierra del Fuego, and elsewhere in the 1830's and published the results in *The Voyage of the Beagle,* 1839. Justus von Liebig, 1803-73—German chemist and teacher.

33 Jean La Pérouse, 1741-88—French explorer who died by shipwreck. Hanno, fl. 500 B.C.—Carthaginian navigator, author of the travel book "Periplus."

34 Neva River—near Leningrad, Russia.

35 Ida Laura Pfeiffer, 1797-1858—Austrian travel writer, author of *A Woman's Journey Round the World,* 1850.

38 Parcae—the three Roman mythological Fates.

42 Samuel Laing, 1810-97—British author and railroad administrator, author of *Journal of a Residence in Norway,* 1836.

44 Daniel Gookin, 1612-87, English- or Irish-born Massachusetts Puritan, author of *Historical Collections of the Indians in New England,* publ. 1792.

46-48 The Biblical references are to Matthew 26:11 and Ezekiel 18:2-4. Thoreau often paraphrases the Bible without using quotation marks (for example, see 105).

50 George Chapman, 1559?-1634?—British playwright and translator of Homer; *Caesar and Pompey,* 1631, V, ii.

51 Momus—Greek fault-finding son of Night. Minerva —Roman goddess of wisdom.

54 Memnon—Egyptian king whose 1st-century B.C. statue emitted a twanging sound when morning sunlight first struck it.

55   Sardanapalus—9th-century B.C. corrupt and effeminate Assyrian king.

57   Edward Johnson, 1598-1672—Massachusetts soldier and historian, author of *A History of New England: From the English Planting in the Yeere 1628 untill the Yeere 1625,* publ. 1654, better known as *The Wonder-Working Providence.*

61   This poem, like all others in *Walden* without quotation marks, is by Thoreau.

73   Cambridge College—Harvard College. Adam Smith, 1723-90; David Ricardo, 1772-1823; Jean Baptiste Say, 1767-1832—economists.

78   Arthur Young, 1741-1820—British agronomist and social economist.

79   Bhagvat-Geeta—*Bagavad-gita,* Thoreau's favorite Oriental literary work, a Hindu scriptural classic. Thebes—ancient Egyptian city of a hundred gates. Vitruvius—1st-century B.C. Roman architect and engineer.

80   Tartar—an Asiatic; most Asiatics believe in the transmigration of souls after death.

85   Marcus Porcius Cato, 234-149 B.C.—Roman statesman whose one extant book is *De Agricultura,* also called *De Re Rustica* (*On Agriculture*).

91   "The evil that . . ."—William Shakespeare, 1564-1616, *Julius Caesar,* 1599, III, ii.

92   William Bartram, 1739-1823—American botanist, ornithologist, painter, and author of *Travels through North and South Carolina, Georgia, and Florida,* 1791.

97   Admetus—when banished from heaven, the god Apollo tended the flocks of King Admetus of Pherae.

103   Robin Goodfellow—mischievous little fairy, also called Puck. Phaëton—son of Helios the Greek sun-god.

104 John Howard, 1726-90—British philanthropist who advocated prison reform.

107 Elizabeth Fry, 1780-1845—British philanthropist and with Howard an advocate of prison reform.

108 Patagonian—person from the southernmost part of South America.

111 Sadi, c. 1184-1291—didactic Persian poet, who wrote *Gulistān,* or "Rose-garden," 1258. Thomas Carew, c. 1598-c. 1639—British courtier poet under Charles I and author of *Coelum Britannicum,* 1634, from which the quotation is taken.

2. *Where I Lived, and What I Lived For*

Thoreau once tramped about the Concord area so thoroughly that many thought he was a real-estate broker. But he was only looking for a farm to buy. In his imagination, he went so far as to refuse possession of several places. Once, he so liked a farm that he was prepared to buy it and even began to sort his seeds for planting, but the owner's wife changed her mind—fortunately. He did like that farm, however, he explains, because of its retired location, its general dilapidated condition, the prevalence of nibbling rabbits, and his memories of happy trips taken some time ago on its nearby river. But then he recalls Cato's advice to the would-be buyer of a farm: "The oftener you go there the more it will please you, if it is good." Thoreau extends this thought and determines to be buried in a pleasant farm first, "that it may please me the more" (6). (1-6)

Now Thoreau begins his experiment. For convenience,

he will compress its two years into one. When he began to live in his little house, it was not quite finished but had wide, un-plastered chinks; hence it was cool at night and dewy in the morning. He was now a neighbor to the birds, by caging him-self near them. He was a mile and a half south of Concord and a little higher, and two miles south of Concord Battle Ground. At especially wet times, Walden Pond and the nearby flooded meadows reminded him that our dry land is indeed insular. In imagination he enjoyed vast horizons and seemed astronomically remote from life left behind him. (7-13)

Especially precious to Thoreau was the morning. Each morning he arose early, awakened by celestial music and fra-grance in the air—never "by the mechanical nudging of some servitor"—and made a religious exercise of bathing. There is something unique about the morning, he says, something epic and divine. At such a time, we ought to be truly awake to life's offerings and aware that we can elevate ourselves by our own conscious efforts. "To be awake is to be alive," Thoreau concludes, then adds, however, "I have never yet met a man who was quite awake" (14). (14-15)

Thoreau went to the woods to simplify, to live essentially, and to learn for himself whether it is true that we are here to glorify God. We should avoid frittering away our strength in details but instead eat only one meal a day perhaps, reduce our affairs, keep our accounts on our thumb-nail, and practice sim-plicity. We think that we cannot have progress, either material or spiritual, without extending our railroads. Meanwhile, we are mindless that "We do not ride on the railroad; it rides on us" (17). And we are too hurried and wasteful. After an hour's nap, a man will ask what the news is. Thoreau, on the other hand, is of the opinion that very few letters are worth their postage and that if one has read one newspaper he has read them all. We mistake shadowy sham for substance, appearance for reality, time for eternity. Thoreau concludes with the suggestion that we all should "spend one day as deliberately as Nature." Only thus can we avoid drifting with the stream of things and instead "work and wedge our feet downward through the mud and slush of opinion, and prejudice, and tradition, and delusion, and appearance," and "come to a hard bottom . . . which we can call *reality*" (22). Then we can agree that time is only a stream to go fishing in, whereas "eternity remains" (23). (16-23)

NOTES

2 "I am monarch . . ."—William Cowper, 1731-1800, "Verses Supposed to Be Written by Alexander Selkirk," 1782; Thoreau italicized *survey* because he was a part-time surveyor.

4 Atlas—in Greek mythology he carried the earth on his shoulders.

6 Cato—see I, 85.

7 Samuel Taylor Coleridge, 1772-1834, wrote an "Ode to Dejection," 1802; Percy Bysshe Shelley, 1792-1822, wrote "Stanzas Written in Dejection, near Naples," 1818.

8 Olympus—mountain residence of the Greek gods.

9 Harivansa—poetic supplement of the ancient Hindu epic poem *Mahabharata*.

12 Damodara—another name for Krishna, Krishna being one of Vishnu's incarnations and hero of the *Mahabharata*.

13 "There was a . . ."—author unknown; the poem was put to music in 1610 by Robert Jones, English lutenist and composer, fl. early 17th century.

14 Aurora—Roman goddess of the dawn. "Renew thyself complete . . ."—Tsang Sin, *The Great Learning*, after Confucius (see I, 15). *Iliad* and *Odyssey*—the two epics of Homer. Vedas—collections of Hindu scriptures. Memnon—see I, 54.

16 "Glorify God and . . ."—from the beginning of the *Westminster Shorter Catechism*.

17 "the fable tells us . . ."—when the island of Oenone was ruined by pestilence, Zeus converted its ants into men called Myrmidons. pygmies and cranes—Homer, *Iliad*, III, compares Greeks to pygmies and Trojans to cranes fighting them. "And if railroads . . ."—one of several allusions in *Walden* to Nathaniel Hawthorne, 1804-64, "The Celestial Railroad," 1843, which portrays new-style pilgrims trying unsuccessfully to get to Heaven in comfort.

18 Wachito River—Ouachita River, in Arkansas. the dark unfathomed mammoth cave . . .—modified from "The dark unfathomed caves of ocean bear," Thomas Gray, 1716-71, "Elegy in a Country Churchyard," 1750; and the Mammoth Cave in Kentucky.

20 "Kieou-he-uy (great dignitary . . .)"—Confucius, *Analects* (see I, 15).

21 Brahme—Brahma in Hindu religion was the supreme and everlasting soul of the universe, and part of the Hindu trinity of Brahma (creator), Vishnu (preserver), and Siva (destroyer).

22 Ulysses—in Homer, *Odyssey*, XII, Ulysses had himself tied by his ear-stopped sailors to the mast so that he could hear the enticing song of Sirens as his boat was rowed past. *point d'appui*—French for "foundation." Nilometer—an instrument for measuring the rise and fall of the Nile River.

3. Reading

One who acquires material goods, a family, or fame is mortal, but whoever seeks the truth is immortal, because he is at one with the oldest Hindu philosopher. Thoreau explains that his residence at Walden favored thought and serious reading more than a university could; even when he labored at his house and at his beans, he sustained himself by the prospect of future happy reading. He kept Homer's *Iliad* nearby but glanced at it only occasionally during the first part of his stay at Walden; when he read some light travel literature to divert himself, he quickly became ashamed and asked himself where he lived. (1-2)

Then Thoreau launches into extravagant praise of the classics, which to be truly appreciated must be read in their original languages. These masterpieces are never old, any more than nature ever is. They are noble, and it requires an almost athletic training to master them. And they are not for the many, but only for the few. Only after the various separate European languages were developed in the Middle Ages did individual and exceptional scholars turn back to Greek and Roman masterpieces to become nobly inspired. Comparing the written works of ancient times, which speak "to the intellect and the heart of mankind" (4), to the eloquence of the orator is like comparing the eternal stars to the passing clouds. The written word is "the choicest of relics" (5), being both intimate and universal at once. The best Greek literature has spread through the world to do battle against the corrosive effects of time. Thoreau next lavishes specific praise upon Homer, Aeschylus, and Virgil, saying that their works are "as refined, as solidly done, and as beautiful almost as the morning." Modern men have a right to say that we should forget the classics only when they have the ability to appreciate them. Add to these classics the Vedas, the Zendavestas, the Bible, Dante, and Shakespeare, and "By such a pile we may hope to scale heaven at last" (6). (3-6)

Unfortunately these great poetic works can be thoroughly read only by poets; ordinary persons read them as they do the stars, "astrologically, not astronomically" (7). Most people learn to read simply to cipher, keep accounts, and avoid being cheated, then at most go on and read "the nine thousandth tale about Zebulon and Sophronia, and how they loved as none had ever loved before," instead of "the best that is in literature" (8). Concord culture is no exception, Thoreau maintains: even college graduates in Concord have little acquaintance with the classics. Thoreau aspires to know wiser minds than Concord has produced, and yet he himself leaves Plato's *Dialogues* on the next shelf, unread. Why do we not seek out those books which "will explain our miracles and reveal new ones" (11)? We boast of our nineteenth-century progress, and yet Concord village does little to develop itself culturally. We should be provoked like oxen, so that we will do more. "We spend more on almost any article of bodily aliment or ailment than on our mental aliment." Concord should institute programs of adult education, hiring distinguished men to lecture and supporting lyceum series. It should surround itself with the best from all realms of culture and learning. "New England can hire all the wise men in the world to come and teach her, and board them round the while, and not be provincial at all" (12). Then it would have uncommon schools and noble villages of men rather than mere noblemen. (7-12)

NOTES

2 Mîr Camar Uddîn Mast—Mîr Qamar-uddīn Minnat, d. 1793, Persian and Urdu poet, lived in India.

3 Delphi and Dondona—ancient Greek oracles.

6 Vedas—see II, 14. Zendavestas—Zendavesta is Zoroas-
trian scripture (Avesta) together with translation and commentary (Zend).

11 Zoroaster—Persian religious reformer who flourished
in prehistoric times, perhaps 7th, 8th, or 9th century B.C.

12 Pierre Abélard, 1079-1142—French theologian and
teacher.

4. Sounds

But better than reading or even working was Thoreau's
joyful sitting in revery at his door. Nature's language was
then before him, to read. He sometimes sat thus all day, "in
undisturbed solitude and stillness," and grew then "like corn
in the night." Instead of singing like a bird, he only chuckled
and warbled at his "incessant good fortune." Men might have
called him idle, "but if the birds and flowers had tried me by
their standards [he adds], I should not have been found wanting" (1). His life thus was amusing and novel at every turn.
Even housekeeping was only a pastime: he would set all his
furniture outside—soon vines would grow round his little writing table's three legs—and scrub his floor with water and white
sand from the pond. All about were pines, hickories, berries,
goldenrod, oaks, cherries, and sumach bending as it grew.
(1-4)

As Thoreau sat by his window one summer afternoon, he
heard hawks, pigeons, frogs, and reed-birds, and then the rattle
of the railroad, "now dying away and then reviving like the

beat of a partridge" (5). The men on the Fitchburg railroad bowed to him as to an old friend. Its whistle would scream like a hawk, and the "engine with its train of cars" would remind him of a comet, "for the beholder knows not if with that velocity and with that direction it will ever revisit this system" (8). Then Thoreau extensively compares the train to an iron horse—snorting, shaking the earth, breathing fire and smoke from its nostrils, sweating clouds of steam, plowing through deep drifts of snow, and taking only brief hours of "iron slumber" (9) in its stable. The train is so regular that men are prompter now and set their clocks by its whistle. Its commerce is so vital that the workers who serve it, who "inhabit the snow-plow for their winter quarters," and who are braver than storms must be admired for their "courage and content" (11). These trains bring Thoreau exotic smells— of palm leaf, manila hemp, coconut husks, Spanish hides, scrap iron, and rusty nails. And out of New England they carry lumber, lime, paper, cloth, and immortal salt fish. Thoreau also notes the shipments of molasses and brandy, cattle and drovers—but not their abandoned dogs. (5-13)

When the cars have rattled past, bearing the restless world with them, Thoreau, "more alone than ever" (14), can listen to distant church bells—from Lincoln, Acton, Bedford, and Concord—and note that when their sound sweeps through pine needles it acquires a harp-like strain. And he can also hear cows lowing, "whip-poor-wills chanting their vespers" (17), screech owls and their Ben Jonsonian scream—"*Oh-o-o-o-o that I never had been bor-r-r-r-n!*" (18), hoot owls' serenades, wagons rumbling—"a sound heard farther than almost any other at night"—and the "*tr-r-r-oonk*" of "aldermanic" (21) bullfrogs. Thoreau was not sure that he ever heard cocks crowing while he was at Walden, but he was tempted while there to keep a cockerel for its music. The sound of this Indian pheasant, once wild, "would put nations on the alert." Finally, Thoreau notes that many sounds were missing at Walden: he had no domestic sounds, such as those of dogs, cats, pigs, hens, churns, spinning wheels, singing kettles, "nor children crying, to comfort [him]." Nor were there rats in his walls, since he had never baited any inside; but he had squirrels, blue jays, hares, woodchucks, geese, and a loon. At Walden there were no yard birds—in fact, "No yard! but unfenced nature reaching up to your very sills. . . . no gate—no front-yard,—and no path to the civilized world" (22). (14-22)

NOTES

1 Puri Indians of Brazil—described by Ida Laura Pfeiffer (see I, 35).

5 "In truth our village . . ."; William Ellery Channing, 1818-1901, "Walden Spring," *The Woodman and Other Poems,* 1849; note the pun on Concord. Channing was one of Thoreau's closest friends and is the poet of XIII, 5, and XIV, 20.

10 Dismal Swamp—in southern Virginia and northern North Carolina, described by William Byrd, 1674-1744, in *The History of the Dividing Line,* 1729, publ. 1841. Atropos— one of the three Greek Fates (see I, 38); she snipped the threads of human life.

11 Buena Vista—scene in northern Mexico of General Zachary Taylor's victory over Santa Anna, February, 1847; Thoreau loathed the Mexican War because it was imperialistic and also had the effect of extending slave territory. Great Snow—that of 1717 or perhaps of 1780.

13 "to be the mast . . ."—John Milton, 1608-74, *Paradise Lost,* 1667, I.

18 u-lu-lu—from Latin *ululo,* "to wail."

21 Stygian—infernal, from Greek mythological River Styx in Hades; in Dante's *Inferno,* VII, the Styx is a swamp.

5. Solitude

Suddenly we are with Thoreau as he describes a delicious
evening, when one's entire body "imbibes delight through
every pore" (1). Thoreau walks in his shirt-sleeves through
the cool air, hears the bullfrogs, sees the ripples on the water,
and notes that never are all the creatures in nature asleep.
When he walks back to his house, cards, bunches of flowers,
or traces of tobacco smoke in the air tell him that in his absence visitors have come and he has missed them.   (1-2)

Thoreau now wonders why he has all this space separating
him from his fellow-men. It is almost as if the very sun and
moon and stars were his private ones. At night no visitors
ever came to his house, except—and this rarely—when a few
came in the spring to fish for pouts. He thinks that all men
are still a little afraid of the dark, "though the witches are
all hung, and Christianity and candles have been introduced"
(3). But Thoreau has experienced an encouraging society in
nature, is a friend of the seasons, dearly loves the rain, and
counts the swelling pine needles his companions. He confesses that once, although for only an hour and that shortly
after coming to Walden, he was oppressed by a sense of loneliness, but he knew at the time that it would pass. Some of his
happiest hours came during long pelting rains when he had
time for thoughts "to take root and unfold themselves." When
men ask him if he ever felt lonesome at Walden, he is always
tempted to point out that the "most distant inhabitants of
yonder star, the breadth of whose disk cannot be appreciated
by our instruments," are relatively close, in addition that we
cannot diminish our essential distance one from another by
walking nearer to each other, and finally that what each of

us should wish to come closest to is surely "the perennial
source of our life" (5). So long as God's influence is near us,
we can certainly do "without the society of our gossips a little
while" (10). By the action of his own thought a person can
stand apart from society, actions, events, nature, and even
himself. (3-11)

Now Thoreau confesses happily that he finds solitude
wholesome and loves to be alone. He adds that "A man thinking or working is always alone" (12). Only after sufficient
solitude has enabled us to acquire a new value should we seek
society again. Meeting others too frequently, he feels, makes us
lose some respect for them. "The value of a man is not in his
skin, that we should touch him" (13). When we are sadly
alone, we can people our solitude by virtue of imagination.
Thoreau then suggests that he is never more companionless
than the solitary loon in his pond, than the lake itself, than
God, or a mullein or dandelion, a bean leaf, sorrel, a fly or
bee, the Mill Brook, the weathercock, or the north star, the
south wind, an April shower, or a January thaw, "or the first
spider in a new house." But, he adds, "the devil, he is far from
being alone; he sees a great deal of company; he is legion"
(15). (12-15)

Rhapsodically, Thoreau concludes by poetically suggesting
that he has two wondrous mythic visitors, "an old settler and
original proprietor, who . . . dug Walden Pond," and an "el-
derly dame . . . in whose odorous herb garden [he] love[s]
to stroll, gathering simples and listening to her fables" (16).
Innocent, beneficent nature can always speak to him, and why
not? "Am I not [he asks] partly leaves and vegetable mould
myself?" (17). Finally, Thoreau reminds us that no patent
medicine vended out of "those long shallow black-schooner
looking wagons" is so invigorating as "a draught of undiluted

morning air." Thoreau is no devotee of Hygeia (health), the daughter of Aesculapius (medicine), but rather of "Hebe, cup-bearer to Jupiter, who was the daughter of Juno and wild lettuce" (18), the only healthy girl in the world: wherever she walked, it was spring. (16-18)

NOTES

3 "the world to darkness . . ."—Gray, "Elegy in a Country Churchyard" (see II, 18).

4 Aeolian—pertaining to wind, from Aeolus, Greek god of the winds. "Mourning untimely consumes . . ."—James Macpherson, 1736-96, *The Genuine Remains of Ossian,* 1760-63, trans. Patrick MacGregor, London, 1841.

7-10 Confucius (see I, 15)—*The Doctrine of the Mean* and *Analects.*

11 Indra—Hindu god of sky, thunder, and rain.

12 dervis—dervish, member of any of several Moslem orders dedicated to poverty and chastity.

15 blue devils—despondency.

16 Edward Whalley, c. 1620-c. 1674, and his son-in-law William Goffe, c. 1605-79—after the Restoration they were indicted for participating in the execution of Charles I; so they escaped to America, hiding in Connecticut and Massachusetts for some time.

18 Thomas Parr, c. 1483-1638—unbelievably aged Britisher (dying at age 152), now buried in Westminster Abbey. Acheron—Greek and Roman mythological river of woe in Hades. Hygeia—Greek goddess of health, daughter of Aesculapius, god of medicine. Hebe—Greek goddess of youth and spring, cup-bearer, reputedly was conceived when her mother Juno ate some lettuce.

6. *Visitors*

Thoreau explains that he is not naturally a hermit and might even become a bar frequenter if his business required it. He had three chairs in his house—"one for solitude, two for friendship, three for society" (2). As many as twenty-five or thirty people visited in his house at one time, which made him conclude that most fancy residences are so large that their inhabitants seem like vermin and mice by comparison. He admits that his house seemed too small sometimes to permit his noble thoughts and those of his guest "to get into sailing trim and run a course or two before they make their port" (3). His best room, his "withdrawing room" (4), was the pine wood behind his house; he took exceptional guests back there. He was always willing to feed his guests when he could, but if twenty people came and sat around until dinner time he said nothing about food. He has been deterred, he interpolates, from visiting at many a home because of "the parade one made about dining [him]" (5). He then summarizes the historical account of an early Plymouth colonist who paid his respects to a tribe of hospitable but impoverished Indians: the man was lodged intimately enough, but nothing was said about eating, since his hosts "were wiser than to think that apologies could supply the place of food" (6). (1-6)

And now Thoreau tells about the visitors he had at his house. There was a French-Canadian woodchopper—simple, natural, healthy, strong but sluggish, tireless and rollickingly good-spirited. He took pride in his work, had the rudiments of an education provided by Catholic priests, but was really less intellectual and spiritual than he was animal. He had thoughts which were sound, but he lacked the ability to express them.

He responded sensibly to questions about such matters as reform, factories, and money. Thoreau could not tell whether
"he was as wise as Shakespeare or as simply ignorant as a
child" (12), but finally compared him to a deep lake—bottomless, dark, and muddy. (7-14)

Half-witted men also came out to see Thoreau. One said
humbly that he was "deficient in intellect. . . . It was the
Lord's will, I suppose" (15), the man added. Some visitors
sought not hospitality but "hospitalality," earnestly wanting
only to be helped. Of them Thoreau says coldly that "Objects
of charity are not guests" and that they "did not know when
their visit had terminated, though I went about my business
again, answering them from greater and greater remoteness."
Then there were runaway slaves, so to speak, including "One
real runaway slave, among the rest," whom Thoreau helped
"toward the north star." Also there were men of a single idea
and men of a thousand ideas—"men of ideas instead of legs,
a sort of intellectual centipede that made you crawl all over"
(16). Finally, many others visited Thoreau at Walden Pond:
glad girls and boys and young women, businessmen, restless
men, ministers—they "spoke of God as if they enjoyed a mo-
nopoly of the subject"—doctors, lawyers, "uneasy housekeepers," "young men who had ceased to be young," the old and
sick and timid—"to them life seemed full of dangers" (17)—
self-appointed reformers, children, railroaders, fishermen, hunters, poets, and philosophers. Thoreau was afraid of being har-
ried by certain visitors, but to "all honest pilgrims" he cried,
"Welcome" (18). (15-18)

NOTES

5 hasty-pudding—corn-meal mush; the subject of the
splendid poem "Hasty Pudding," 1796, by Joel Barlow, 1754-
1812. Cerberus—Greek and Roman mythological three-headed

dog guarding the gates of Hades. Edmund Spenser, 1552?-99, *Faerie Queene,* 1589, 1596, I, i.

6 Edward Winslow, 1595-1655—English-born American colonial historian and governor, evidently with William Bradford the author of *Journal of the Beginning and Proceedings of the English Plantation at Plymouth,* 1622, also called *Mourt's Relation.* Massasoit, d. 1661—a Wampanoag Indian chief in the Massachusetts and Rhode Island area who made a treaty with the colonists in 1621.

8 Canadian woodchopper—identified as Alex Therien. Paphlagonian—an inhabitant of an ancient Roman province south of the Black Sea. "Or have you . . ."—Homer, *Iliad,* XVI.

13 *pecunia*—Latin for "money," from *pecus,* "cattle."

7. The Bean-Field

Meanwhile, Thoreau planted and hoed rows of beans totaling seven miles. He loved them, since they attached him to the earth so that he got strength like Antaeus. He was aided by dew, rain, the sun, and the soil's fertility. His happiest thought was that he was now here at Walden Pond, growing beans and occasionally playing his flute, at the very spot through which at the age of four he had been taken from Boston back to his native Concord. (1-2)

He now explains his husbandry. He planted 2½ acres of beans, starting about the first of June, in rows three feet by eighteen inches apart. He used no manure, since the land had been cleared only fifteen years earlier. He hoed weeds—"dabbling like a plastic artist in the dewy and crumbling sand"

(4)—while the dew was on them. He tossed dust on their ruined heads. "Daily the beans saw me come to their rescue armed with a hoe, and thin the ranks of their enemies, filling up the trenches with weedy dead. Many a lusty crest-waving Hector, that towered a whole foot above his crowding comrades, fell before my weapon and rolled in the dust" (9). He rested in an oak copse at one end of his fifteen-rod rows and at the other in a berry field, "where the green berries deepened their tints by the time I had made another bout" (4). It amused him to overhear travelers who passed near his fields gossiping adversely upon him. A more Paganini-like accompaniment to his work was the singing of the brown thrasher high in the birch above. Occasion for philosophizing was his frequently disturbing "the ashes of unchronicled nations who in primeval years lived under these heavens, and their small implements of war and hunting [which] were brought to the light of this modern day." More entertainment was provided by hawks circling overhead, wild pigeons and their "quivering winnowing sound," and outlandishly spotted salamanders—"a trace of Egypt and the Nile" (5)—turned up from rotten stumps. In contrast to Thoreau's peaceful husbandry was martial music occasionally drifting out to the pond from the village, where soldiers were training, marching, and firing guns. Thoreau ironically reports: "I felt proud to know that the liberties of Massachusetts and of our fatherland were in such safe keeping; and as I turned to my hoeing again I was filled with an inexhaustible confidence, and pursued my labor cheerfully with a calm trust in the future" (7). Sometimes the bellows-like expansion and collapse of the military din was so noble and inspiring that he felt like spitting a Mexican, but he stayed with his beans. The hardest part of his labor was selling his harvest, since, as he says, "I came to love my rows, my beans, though so many more than I wanted" (1). His expenses in husbandry were $14.72½, his income from sales $23.44, and therefore his profit $8.71½. (1-13)

Thoreau concludes this chapter by promising to plant "sincerity, truth, simplicity, faith, innocence, and the like" another summer, "if the seed is not lost." Should we not be concerned, he asks, "about a new generation of men" (14) rather than more old crops in New England? Farming is no longer "a sacred art"; farmers, no longer joyful and heroic, because they are now concerned only with ever-larger farms and crops. Therefore today the farmer "leads the meanest of lives. He knows Nature but as a robber" (15). We all forget that from the vantage point of the sun our cultivated fields make only a small part of "the glorious picture" (16) of fields, prairies, and forests. Thoreau may grow a few beans for men, but nature fills the granaries of all living creatures. (14-16)

NOTES

1 Antaeus—Greek mythological wrestler whom Hercules defeated by lifting him above the earth, his source of strength.

4 *agricola laboriosus*—Latin for "a laboring farmer." Henry Coleman, 1785-1849—published surveys of Massachusetts agriculture. *Ranz des Vaches*—any of several Swiss cattle-calling songs. Nicolò Paganini, 1784-1840—famous Italian violin virtuoso; he astonished audiences by playing on the fourth string alone.

6 *tintinnabulum*—Latin for "bell, signal-bell"; used by Juvenal, Plautus, and several others, but not by Virgil; the word does not appear in Monroe Nichols Wetmore, *Index Verborum Vergilianus* (New Haven: Yale University Press, 1911). Perhaps Thoreau was also thinking of Edgar Allan Poe's "tintinnabulation," in "The Bells," 1849.

8 spit a Mexican—an ironic allusion to the patriotic fervor generated by the Mexican War, which Thoreau loathed (see IV, 11).

9 crane—Homer, *Iliad*, III (see II, 17). Hector—the noble Trojan soldier killed by Achilles, at which time the fallen Hector was dragged in the dust (*Iliad*, XXII).

10 Pythagorean—pertaining to Pythagoras, 6th-century B.C. Greek mathematician and philosopher who urged his followers to avoid eating beans. Evelyn—*Discourse of Earth* (see I, 12). Sir Kenelm Digby, 1603-65—author, naval officer, diplomat, and organic chemist; he demonstrated that plants require oxygen.

12 patremfamilias vendacem . . .—Latin for "the head of the family ought to be fond of selling rather than fond of buying" (from Cato [see I, 85]).

14 "And as he . . ."—Francis Quarles, 1592-1644, "The Shepherd's Oracles," 1646.

15 Cato—see I, 85. Marcus Terentius Varro, 116-27 B.C. —Roman soldier and author of many works, including *Rerum Rusticarum* (*On Agriculture*). Ceres—Roman goddess of harvests. Jove or Jupiter—Roman god of earth. Plutus— blinded Greek god of riches. Saturn—Roman god of agriculture; when dethroned by Jupiter, he went to Italy and instructed the people there in agricultural matters.

8. The Village

Thoreau made it a habit to stroll to the village every day or two, to take a little gossip "in homoeopathic doses." Just as he liked to visit a colony of muskrats in one direction from his house, so he occasionally enjoyed "seeing a village of busy men, as curious . . . as if they had been prairie-dogs, each sitting at the mouth of its burrow, or running over to a neighbor's to gossip." He notes that the centers of chatter in the village are the grocery, the bar, the post-office, and the bank. Getting through town was often a little like running a gauntlet; sometimes he had to bolt suddenly, go through a gap in a fence, and so escape to his woods again. (1)

He always found it pleasant, after a stay in town, to launch himself into the darkness, set sail "with a merry crew of thoughts" and only his "outer man at the helm," and so make it to his "snug harbor in the woods." It was always easy to get lost in those woods at night or during a snow-storm, but doing so was pleasant because only then "do we appreciate the vastness and strangeness of nature." (2)

Thoreau alludes briefly to his being arrested while at Walden for refusing to pay his taxes to a state "which buys and sells men, women, and children, like cattle, at the door of its senate-house." He had gone to the woods for other commerce, but representatives of the state came after him to "paw him with their dirty institutions"; no other persons ever molested him, even though he left everything except his papers unlocked and once even journeyed from Walden for two weeks of camping in the Maine woods. He concludes from this as follows: "if all men were to live as simply as I then did, thieving and robbery would be unknown." (3)

NOTES

1 Etesian—northerly Mediterranean summer winds. Orpheus—in Apollonius of Rhodes, 3rd-2nd century B.C. Greek poet, who wrote the *Argonautica,* Orpheus accompanied the Argonauts when they sought the Golden Fleece and saved them once by outsinging the Sirens.

3 One afternoon . . . jail—Thoreau was arrested in July, 1846, in the middle of his second (not first) Walden summer, for refusing to pay taxes to a government permitting the Mexican War, which would have the effect of extending southern slave territory; Thoreau wrote of the entire experience in his "Resistance to Civil Government," published 1849 and later called "Civil Disobedience." woods of Maine—Thoreau traveled to and in Maine early in September, 1846. "Nec bella fuerunt . . ."—Albius Tibullus, 54?-18? B.C., Latin poet, *Elegies*. "You who govern . . ."—Confucius, *Analects* (see I, 15).

9. The Ponds

On the basis of his experience in the hills around Walden Pond, Thoreau would conclude that huckleberries never reach Boston, since their "ambrosial and essential part . . . is lost with the bloom which is rubbed off in the market cart, and they become mere provender" (1). In addition to picking berries, he fished, often with some impatient companion, and in the evenings played his flute in the boat and recalled fishing when younger with fire at night. When living at Walden later, he sometimes angled at midnight memorably. While doing so he would drift in thought into cosmogonal spheres and then be linked to nature by the jerk of a fish on his line. "It seemed as if I might next cast my line upward . . . as well as downward . . . Thus I caught two fishes as it were with one hook" (4). (1-4)

Thoreau now reports some facts concerning Walden Pond. It is half a mile long, a mile and three-quarters around, and

61½ acres. The surrounding wooded hills rise forty to eighty feet near the pond, and much higher than that a few hundred yards to the southeast and to the east. The water varies in color, being blue from a distance, dark slate when stormy, and often green and even yellowish. Whereas the Concord River water is dark and will yellow a bather, "this water is of . . . crystalline purity" (5) and the lake bottom can be seen twenty-five or thirty feet down. One winter Thoreau dropped an axe into the pond by chancing to slide it over the ice and into a fishing hole; with a slip-noose he retrieved it from twenty-five feet of clear water. The bottom has only heart-leaves, potamogetons, and water-targets. Only White Pond, 2½ miles west, is as pure and well-like. Walden "is a gem of the first water which Concord wears in her coronet" (8), and perhaps it is older than the Fall of Man. People from times immemorial have left traces around it: there is a shelf-like path all about it, which light snows make distinct to one standing on the ice in the middle of the pond. The rise and fall of Walden are definite but whether regular or not none knows. Thoreau has seen the level both a foot or two lower and five feet higher. The rise is useful, because it nibbles off shrubs and trees which have sprung up near its edge since the last rise: "thus the *shore* is *shorn* . . . These are the lips of the lake, on which no beard grows. It licks its chaps from time to time" (11). There are delightful legends concerning the presence of a belt of rounded white stones like paving-stones about the pond, but since Thoreau has "observe[d] that the surrounding hills are remarkably full of the same kind of stone," he "detect[s] the paver" (12). Walden water is always cool and tastes good even when it is a week old. The pond yields good pickerel—one was caught which weighed seven pounds and one got away weighing eight—perch, pouts, shiners, chivins, breams, and eels. Walden fish are "cleaner, handsomer, and firmer-fleshed than those in the river and most other ponds, as the water is purer." Clean also are Walden frogs, tortoises, mussels, muskrats, minks, and turtles. Ducks, geese, white-bellied swallows, peetweets, fish hawks, and "one annual loon" (14) also favor Thoreau's pond. In fairly shallow water there are mysterious circular heaps six feet in diameter made of small round stones carefully placed in the sandy bottom. The shore is pleasingly irregular—indented at the west, bold at the north, and scalloped at the south. Seen from the middle of the lake, the woody shore-line has no rawness or imperfection such as an axe causes: "There Nature has woven a natural selvage" (16). A lake is "earth's eye" (17). Walden's surface on a calm September afternoon is literally like glass "except where the skater insects . . . by their motions in the sun produce the finest imaginable sparkle." It is also rewarding to contemplate the swallow skimming, the silvery arc of leaping fish, or a water-bug a quarter of a mile off. These lines of beauty on the calm water are "the constant welling up of its fountain, the gentle pulsing of its life, the heaving of its breast" (18). The surface in September or October is a mirror, undefiled, never cracked, never worn, ever in repair, ever fresh; no breath stains it, but its breath rises to float as clouds above it. The lake mediates between land and sky. But late in October and in November its surface is disturbed by thousands of tiny perch "apparently improving the short season before winter would draw an icy shutter over their broad skylight" (21). An old man told Thoreau that long ago Walden was alive with ducks and eagles, and that there was an old log canoe which was owned by no one but the lake itself. Before the Revolution, there was supposed to be an old iron chest which would float to the shore and then disappear in the depths again. When Thoreau was a boy, Walden was thickly surrounded by pines, oaks, and grape-vines; he used to row out and daydream staring into the sky until roused by the boat grinding the sand at some shore. "I was rich, if not in money, in sunny hours and summer days, and spent them lavishly; nor do I regret that I did not waste more of them in the workshop or the teacher's desk." But since his youth, woodchoppers have ravaged the shores, and now his Muse is silent. "How can you expect the birds to sing when their groves are cut down?" (23). Commercial men in Concord have been thinking of piping Ganges-like Walden water into town. Already the railroad, "That devilish Iron Horse, . . . has browsed off all the woods on Walden shore, that Trojan horse, with a thousand men in his belly, introduced by mercenary Greeks!" (24). But though many are the changes, "Walden wears best, and best preserves its purity" (25), in spite of woodchoppers, Irish sty-builders, railroaders, and icemen. Surely Walden was rounded by God's hand, deepened and clarified by God's thought, and given to Concord by God's will. Railroad cars never look at Walden, but the railroaders themselves, who see it often, are better for the sight. The pond seemingly has no inlet or outlet, but it is related to Flint's Pond to the east and higher, and to Concord River lower in the west. However, Walden has acquired purity because of its reserve and austerity, "like a hermit in the woods" (27). (5-27)

Now for the ponds nearby. Flint's Pond, or Sandy Pond, a mile east of Walden, is larger, more fertile in fish, shallower, and less pure. Thoreau then rages at the stupidity of naming it Flint's Pond after an "unclean and stupid farmer," a "skinflint, who loved better the reflecting surface of a dollar, or a bright cent, in which he could see his own brazen face; who regarded even the wild ducks which settled in it as trespassers; his fingers grown into crooked and horny talons from the long habit of grasping harpy-like." Such people would drain a pond and sell the mud at its bottom, would carry the landscape, would carry their God, to market. "Farmers are respectable and interesting to me [Thoreau continues violently] in proportion as they are poor,—poor farmers. A modern farm! where the house stands like a fungus in a muck-heap, chambers for men, horses, oxen, and swine, cleansed and uncleansed, all contiguous to one another! Stocked with men! A great grease-spot, redolent of manures and buttermilk! Under a high state of cultivation, being manured with the hearts and brains of men! As if you were to raise your potatoes in the churchyard! Such is a model farm" (29). No, Thoreau concludes, let us name things in nature only after the noblest of men. (28-30)

Goose Pond is next, then Fair Haven—a part of Concord River—and then White Pond, perhaps so named for its pure water or perhaps for the color of its sand. In a way White Pond is a smaller twin of Walden. Thoreau says that White Pond might be called Yellow Pine Lake, since fifteen years earlier one might have seen the top of a pitch pine projecting from its surface. A 1792 topographical description of the Concord area reported the tree, but in 1849 Thoreau talked with a man who had cut a channel in the ice of the frozen pond for a dozen rods from shore to it in thirty or forty feet of water, and then hauling it out with oxen discovered it to be upside down with its small end firm in the sandy bottom. It had been there eighty years or more. Having few fish, White Pond has rarely been "profaned by a boat." Thoreau concludes by comparing Walden Pond and White Pond to precious gems which, "being liquid and ample, and secured to us and our successors forever, we disregard . . . and run after the diamond of Kohinoor" (34). Both lakes are beautiful, transparent, unappreciated, wild, and pure. (31-34)

NOTES

1 "to fresh woods . . ."—Milton (see IV, 13), "Lycidas," 1637. three hills—Boston, originally built on three hills, was once called Tremont.

8 Castalian Fountain—a spring on Mount Parnassus sacred to Apollo and the Muses.

11 ancient settler—see IX, 11.

14 *reticulatus*—Latin for "like a small net." *guttatus*—Latin for "spotted, speckled."

18 murder will out—Geoffrey Chaucer, c. 1340-1400, "The Prioress's Tale," *The Canterbury Tales,* c. 1387; Miguel de Cervantes Saavedra, 1547-1616, *Don Quixote,* I (1605), iii, 8.

24 Trojan horse—Virgil, 70-19 B.C., *Aeneid,* II; the Greeks defeated the Trojans by leaving on the beach a soldier-filled wooden horse which the Trojans then broke down their wall to take into the city. Moore of Moore Hall—modified from the ballad "The Dragon of Wantley," in Bishop Thomas Percy, 1729-1811, ed., *Reliques of Ancient English Poetry,* 1765.

27 waste its sweetness . . .—modified from "And waste its sweetness on the desert air," Gray, "Elegy in a Country Churchyard" (see II, 18).

30 Icarian Sea—from Icarus, Greek mythological character who flew with wax-glued wings so high that the sun melted off his wings and he fell into the Aegean Sea. "still the shore," etc.—William Drummond of Hawthornden, 1585-1649, "Icarus," 1616.

34 Kohinoor—Koh-i-Nor ("Mountain of Light"), an Indian diamond with a history going back to the 14th century; in 1849, when Great Britain annexed the Punjab, northwest India, Queen Victoria acquired the 186-carat gem as a crown jewel.

10. Baker Farm

Thoreau often walked through the woods, which were "standing like temples," to inspect the blueberries, juniper, swamps, lichen, spruce, toadstools, fungi, swamp-pink, dogwood, alderberries, and holly. Instead of calling on certain scholars, he visited particular birch and beech trees, and bass, hornbeams, elms, and pagoda-like hemlocks. "These were the shrines I visited both summer and winter" (1). Once he stood, he claims, at the foot of a dazzling rainbow. Often, as he walked along the railroad causeway, he noted a halo of light around the shadow of his head, which sight reminded him of Cellini's similar boast. (1-2)

One afternoon, planning to fish at Fair Haven, he walked through an adjunct of Baker Farm, was caught in a shower, and therefore sought shelter in the leaky hut of John Field, an Irish tenant farmer, his wife, several children—including a helpful, broad-faced son and a "sibyl-like, cone-headed infant"—and familiar chickens—"too humanized, methought, to roast well." To Field, Thoreau explained that he dressed lightly, worked very little, and hence needed no tea or coffee, dairy products, or meat, or heavy boots. Field and his wife were unable to revise their wretched mode of existence, however, and "therefore I suppose [Thoreau concludes] they still take life bravely, after their fashion, face to face, giving it tooth and nail, not having skill to split its massive columns with any fine entering wedge, and rout it in detail" (3).When the rain quit and Thoreau was about to leave, he asked for some water, hoping thus to complete his inspection by seeing the well, which, however, was not in working order. But they agreeably gave him some warm and muddy water: "Such gruel sustains life here, I thought; so, shutting my eyes, and excluding the motes by a skilfully directed undercurrent, I drank to genuine hospitality the heartiest draught I could" (5). (3-5)

As Thoreau left, it suddenly occurred to him that he was wasting his time and college education wading through bog-holes for pickerel. But the red west ahead, and the rainbow behind him, and tinkling sounds wafted through the washed air all inspired him anew to remember his God, abandon care, love his own locale, earn his little as though at sport, and laugh at tradesmen who live like serfs. Most men came home at night tamely after routine labor, "and their life pines because it breathes its own breath over again . . ." But, Thoreau concludes, "We should come home from afar, from adventures, and perils, and discoveries each day, with new experience and character" (8). (6-8)

As a kind of postscript, Thoreau reports briefly that John Field followed him out and fished with him. "But he, poor man, disturbed only a couple of fins while I was catching a fair string, and he said it was his luck . . ." When they changed seats in the boat, "luck changed seats too" (9). Poor Field had left poverty-stricken Ireland for what he thought would be liberty in America. "But the only true America is that country where you are at liberty to pursue such a mode of life as may enable you to do without these [expensive foods], and where the state does not endeavor to compel you to sustain the slavery and war and other superfluous expenses which directly and indirectly result from the use of such things" (3).

NOTES

1 Druids—members of ancient Celtic religious orders, whose downfall was caused by the advent of Romans in the British Isles. Valhalla—Norse mythological hall to which go the souls of heroes killed in war.

2 Benvenuto Cellini, 1500-71—Italian goldsmith, sculptor,

and egocentric autobiographer, once imprisoned in the Castle
of St. Angelo (originally Hadrian's tomb) near the Tiber River
in Rome.

3 "Thy entry is . . ."—Channing (see IV, 5), "Baker
Farm" (1849), in *Thoreau, the Poet-Naturalist,* 1873, rev. 1902.
"And here a poet . . ."—Channing, "Baker Farm."

7 "Landscape where the . . ."—Channing, "Baker Farm."

9 *talaria*—Roman mythological winged shoes attached
to the ankles.

11. *Higher Laws*

Coming home with his fish, Thoreau goes on, he saw a
woodchuck and was tempted to seize and devour him raw.
He remembers ranging the woods occasionally like a starving
dog, at which times no food would have been too wild. All
of this makes him realize that he has both a primitive, savage
side and a higher, spiritual one. He reverences both. He thinks
that his former love of hunting when young accounts for his
lower nature now; and, though he has now sold his gun, he
recalls fishing from dire necessity often. He goes on to record
his approval of the sport of hunting, as educational. He pities
the boy who has never gone fowling and adds that almost
every youth outgrows the sport and then ceases "wantonly
murder[ing] any creature which holds its life by the same
tenure that he does" (3). By then the young man has been
happily introduced to forest and pond by gun and pole. The
only employment that now takes most grown men to lovely
Walden, aside from businesses like wood and ice gathering,
is fishing; but habitually they become "too old and dignified

to go a-fishing, and so they know it no more forever. Yet even they expect to go to heaven at last" (4). (1-4)

Next Thoreau confesses that of late he cannot fish without losing a little self-respect, skillful though he is at enjoyable angling. He feels increasingly that there is something unclean about a fishy diet and indeed all flesh for food. He knows what he is talking about since he has been butcher, scullion, and cook, as well as the served gentleman. Animal food is unclean. Fish do not feed him essentially. Bread and potatoes would do as well, with less inconvenience. He goes on to asseverate that everyone anxious "to preserve his higher or poetic faculties . . . has been particularly inclined to abstain from animal food." A "gross feeder" (5) is like a voracious larva, a caterpillar, or a maggot; the more spiritual feeder is like a butterfly or fly. When food is prepared for a person, it feeds—and often offends—his imagination as well as his body. If people were obliged personally to prepare the food they eat which other hands prepare, they would modify their diet in shame. As mankind evolves, it will undoubtedly "leave off eating animals, as surely as the savage tribes have left off eating each other when they came in contact with the more civilized" (6). We should be willing to desist from brutalizing food even if it means bodily weakness, because doing so would be a triumph of higher principles. Thoreau boasts that he was never squeamish and could eat a fried rat with relish if necessary, but he immediately adds that water is the only drink for the wise man and pure air the best intoxicant. Coarse labor compels one to eat and drink coarsely also, and Thoreau confesses to a certain increase in his own coarseness over the years. But surely it is better to savor one's food delicately rather than grossly, for thus one lets it feed the soul and not the gluttonous animal part. Gluttony is produced by the gross appetite with which one approaches any food and not by the kind of food one eats. A hunter with a taste for "savage tidbits" like mud-turtles and muskrats may defile himself less than "the fine lady [who sensually] indulges a taste for jelly made of a calf's foot, or for sardines from over the sea." Thoreau concludes by wondering in revulsion how we all "can live this slimy, beastly life, eating and drinking" (9). (5-9)

We are the battleground for virtue and vice, between which there is no truce. We are aware of the sensual animal in us, but we should suppress it and command our passions. "The generative energy, which, when we are loose, dissipates and makes us unclean, when we are continent invigorates and inspires us. Chastity is the flowering of man; and what are called Genius, Heroism, Holiness, and the like, are but various fruits which succeed it. Man flows at once to God when the channel of purity is open. By turns our purity inspires and our impurity casts us down. He is blessed who is assured that the animal is dying out in him day by day, and the divine being established." Thoreau expresses his fears "that we are such gods or demigods only as fauns and satyrs, the divine allied to beasts, the creatures of appetites, and that, to some extent, our very life is our disgrace" (11). Next he suggests that "All sensuality is one . . . [and] all purity is one." A person can be sensual in eating, drinking, cohabiting, and even sleeping. "If you would be chaste, you must be temperate" (12) and work earnestly, from which habits of life come wisdom and purity, while from immoderation and sloth come all sensuality. Unfortunately, we are so degraded that we cannot now speak of necessary bodily functions—such as reproduction and elimination—without shame. But the Hindu lawgiver could and did, teaching all elements of life and "elevating what is mean" (13). We should realize with him that every man in developing or degrading his body builds a temple, noble or sensual. "Any nobleness begins at once to refine a man's features, and meanness or sensuality to imbrute them" (14). (10-14)

Thoreau concludes with a muted little parable. John Farmer, exhausted after his hard day's work, sat resting at his door one September evening, and suddenly heard flute notes floating through the cool air. He still thought of his work, but the music told him of other ideas and "suggested work for certain faculties which slumbered in him." And a voice seemed to ask him why he toiled like a beast when a more glorious way was near. (15)

NOTES

3 "yave not of the text . . ."—slightly modified from Chaucer, "Prologue," *Canterbury Tales* (see IX, 18); Chaucer wrote this of a monk, however, not a nun.

5 William Kirby (1759-1850) and William Spence (1783-1860), *An Introduction to Entomology,* 1815-26.

8 Ved—Rajah Rammohun Roy, trans., *Translation of Several . . . of the Veds,* 1832—for Ved, see II, 14. Vedant—Vedantist, one conversant with the Veds.

9 "The soul not . . ."—Tsang Sin, *The Great Learning* (see II, 14).

11 "That in which . . ."—*Works of Mencius,* IV; Mencius, d. 289? B.C., Chinese philosopher. "A command over . . ."—*Translation of Several . . . of the Veds* (see 8 above). "How happy's he . . ."—John Donne, 1572-1631, "To Sr Edward Herbert. at Iulyers," 1633 ms.

12. *Brute Neighbors*

Thoreau casts in the form of a dialogue his encounter
with a fishing companion. He calls himself the Hermit and
his friend the Poet. The Hermit begins by noting the farmer's
noon horn, which calls the tired hands to their heavy meal
of beef, cider, and bread, necessarily heavy because the eaters
have been exhausted by their work. The Hermit then asks
the Poet how he likes everything today. The Poet comments
on the beauty of the clouds and adds that they resemble Spanish clouds in a Mediterranean sky. He then invites the Hermit
to join him at fishing. The Hermit is willing but says that he
has a little more meditating to accomplish and therefore the
Poet can go and dig the angleworms for bait. Then the Hermit tries sadly and unsuccessfully to recapture his vanished
thoughts, concluding that "There never is but one opportunity
of a kind" (5). When the Poet returns with sufficient bait,
the two go off to Concord River. (1-7)

Now Thoreau describes the kinds and activities of the
wild life about him at Walden. Together the various species
make a little world. He has unusual mice, unlike any found in
the village and very tame. He has phoebes, robins, and partridges. He describes in detail the ability of tiny partridges to
play dead while the mother tries to attract a person's attention
away from them. He has seen raccoons and probably heard their
"whinnering at night." He likes the "faint, wiry peep" (11)
of the woodcock, and likes also the turtle doves and red squirrels. But more absorbing was an epic fight he once saw and
precisely studied between a small red ant and a large black
ant. Suddenly, to aid his confrere, a second red ant rapidly
approached and "sprang upon the black warrior, and com-
menced his operations near the root of his right fore leg,

leaving the foe to select among his own members." Thoreau half expected to see a military band of ants come up "to excite the slow and cheer the dying combatants" (12). The engagement between the Redcoats and the Patriots at Concord was nothing compared to Homeric ant wars such as Thoreau saw. He transferred the three mortally struggling ants on their chip to his window-sill and watched until "the black soldier had severed the heads of his foes from their bodies, and the still living heads were hanging from either side of him like ghastly trophies at his saddle-bow, still apparently as firmly fastened as ever, and he was endeavoring with feeble struggles, being without feelers and with only a remnant of a leg, and I know not how many wounds, to divest himself of them" (13). Thoreau then digresses on the subject of historical accounts of ant warfare. Then he explains that while heavy village dogs make poor hunters in the woods, a village cat, no matter how pampered, turns atavistically feline when placed there. He recalls the legend of a winged cat in nearby Lincoln: it had hunted in the woods and accordingly developed thick, flat strips of fur like wings along her sides. But the most intriguing brute neighbor was a loon—*Colymbus glacialis*—which especially in October used to elude Thoreau's most canny and prolonged pursuit by rowboat: "again and again, when I was straining my eyes over the surface one way, I would suddenly be startled by his unearthly laugh behind me. But why, after displaying so much cunning, did he invariably betray himself the moment he came up by that loud laugh? Did not his white breast enough betray him? He was indeed a silly loon, I thought. I could commonly hear the plash of the water when he came up, and so also detected him. But after an hour he seemed as fresh as ever, dived as willingly, and swam yet farther than at first." Often the loon's laugh sounded a little like a water-fowl's note and occasionally like the "long-drawn unearthly howl" of a wolf—"This was his looning,—perhaps the wildest sound that is ever heard here, making the woods ring far and wide" (17). Once in a while, from a successfully great distance away from Thoreau's boat, the loon would emerge and prolongedly howl "as if calling on the god of loons to aid him." Immediately a wind would rise, ripple the pond's surface, and bring a protective misty rain, "as if it were the prayer of the loon answered, and his god was angry with me" (17). (8-17)

Thoreau concludes with a description of the ducks in the fall rising from the pond, circling high enough to see nearby lakes, but then slantingly returning to Walden, undoubtedly because "they love its water for the same reason that I do" (18).

NOTES

1 companion—undoubtedly Channing (see X, 3) rather than Emerson.

8 Pilpay—Bidpai, supposed author of a group of fables stemming from East India, the ultimate source of which is the Sanskrit *Panchatantra.*

9 distinguished naturalist—Louis Agassiz, 1807-73, Swiss-born scientist who came to America in 1846; from 1848 on, he was professor of natural history at Harvard.

12 Myrmidons—Thessalian soldiers under Achilles; at the outset of the Trojan War he sulked in resentment against Agamemnon until Patroclus, Achilles's darling, was killed (*Iliad,* XVI).

13 Hôtel des Invalides—veterans' hospital in Paris, now the location of the tomb of Napoleon.

14 Kirby and Spence—see XI, 5. François Huber, 1750-1831—Swiss naturalist whose specialization was bees. Aeneas Sylvius Piccolomini, 1405-64—was Pope Pius II (1458-64).

Eugenius IV, 1383-1447—was pope from 1431 until his death.
Olaus Magnus, 1490-1558—Swedish ecclesiast and writer, long
a scholar in Rome. Christiern or Christian II, 1481-1559—
brilliant but cruel king of Denmark and Norway (1514-23)
and of Sweden (1520-23). James Polk, 1795-1849—U.S. Presi-
dent 1845-49. Daniel Webster, 1782-1852—American statesman
and oratorical defender of but not author of the Fugitive-Slave
Law.

13. *House-Warming*

In October Thoreau admired the cranberries—ruthlessly
raked off by mercenary farmers concerned only with "the
bushel and the dollar"—and gathered wild grapes and apples,
chestnuts—"a good substitute for bread"—and even groundnuts. He philosophizes that groundnuts, "the potato of the
aborigines," have all but disappeared because of modern civilized farming, but that they cling to life and "seemed like a
faint promise of Nature to rear her own children and feed
them simply here at some future period" (1). Week by week
the scarlet of the maples deepened: "Each morning the man-
ager of the gallery substituted some new picture, distinguished
by more brilliant or harmonious coloring, for the old upon the
walls" (2). As October gave way to November, the more and
more numbed wasps, which often unmolestingly bedded with
Thoreau, began to disappear into their winter quarters; but
Thoreau sought out the remnants of sunlight at the north-
eastern side of Walden, saying, "I thus warmed myself by the
still glowing embers which the summer, like a departed hunter, had left" (4). He built his chimney deliberately, because

he enjoyed the work and because the chimney of a house is independent, pointing to heaven and often surviving the fire which destroys the house. He finished the chimney in November. (1-5)

As Walden began to freeze over, Thoreau plastered his walls against the cold. The plastered house never pleased his eye so much as the bare, knotty walls and the rafters with the bark left on them. But the house was warmer after being plastered. Thoreau was pleased with his single functional room and rejoiced Cato-like in his modestly but adequately stocked little cellar. Sometimes he dreamed of a larger house, which would be "a vast, rude, substantial, primitive hall" (7). There he could offer true hospitality to the weary traveler, who could wash, eat, converse, and sleep once he had merely stepped inside the simple door. Now most people consider hospitality to be the art of keeping a guest at the greatest distance from the host. Thoreau would willingly visit a king and queen in a simple house of the sort he dreams of, but the only gesture he would want to learn before visiting a modern palace is that of backing out of it. Further, most people have lost the art of parlor conversation, which is degenerating into mere palaver; this is so because such language is remote from kitchen and workshop, in fact from nature and truth. Thoreau wryly adds that almost none of his guests stayed to share his hasty-pudding in his house, and yet the house survived many hasty-puddings. (6-9)

Thoreau enjoyed plastering his house in the freezing weather, nailing his laths vigorously and learning a great deal about "the economy and convenience of plastering." He recalled the fate of a conceited villager who, after giving advice to plasterers he was watching, ventured to show them how and then dropped a trowel-full of plaster "in his ruffled bosom." And Thoreau also remembered making lime by burning shells from the river the previous winter, for which reason he omitted this experiment while at Walden. (10)

And now the pond began to freeze steadily. Thoreau lay on the first ice to study the lake bottom as through a glass. He measured the air bubbles in the ice and noted their different sizes and shapes. Some were "like a string of beads" and others "like silvery coins poured from a bag." He experimented by breaking the thickening ice with heavy rocks and studying the way in which it healed. (11)

His plastering done, winter followed in earnest. Nightly Thoreau heard the lumbering geese on their way to Mexico. As Walden froze over completely, he tells us, "I withdrew yet farther into my shell, and endeavored to keep a bright fire both within my house and within my breast." He burned dead wood from the forest, an old fence—sacrificing it "to Vulcan, for it was past serving the god Terminus" (12)—driftwood, and a pine raft made by some Irish railroaders. He respected the living wood, was saddened by any wanton destruction of it, and even "grieved when it was cut down by the proprietors themselves. I would [he continues] that our farmers when they cut down a forest felt some of that awe which the old Romans did when they came to thin, or let in the light to, a consecrated grove (*lucem conlucare*) . . ." (13). Thoreau then discusses the efficiency of various fuels. We all love wood, and it is always essential. A man looks at his wood-pile with affection. Thoreau's warmed him twice, once when he cut it, and again when he burned it. He likes fat pine, stumps of which he prospected for long after the woodchoppers. He used forest leaves for kindling, long stored in his shed for this purpose, and split green hickory, and also burned freshly cut hard green wood. When he temporarily left his house, he often left a fire behind as "a cheerful housekeeper . . . It was I and Fire that lived there" (17). Some friends were surprised that he took such pains for a comfortable fire, speaking to him, he adds, "as if I was coming to the woods on purpose to freeze myself." This makes him philosophize that man, a superior animal, builds a house as an extension of his body and then warms the place as "a kind of summer in the midst of winter" (18), whereas animals make winter beds and warm only them with their bodies. Thoreau adds that the most luxurious houses could not preserve human life if nature decided to blast them with cold only a little sharper than what we have now. And then he concludes by mentioning his discontent with a cook-stove which he used during his second winter: it made cooking merely a chemical process and no longer a poetic one, it took up too much room, it smelled up his house, and it so concealed the fire that, as he says, "I felt as if I had lost a companion" (19). (12-19)

NOTES

1 Ceres—see VII, 15. Minerva—see I, 51.

5 Nebuchadnezzar—King of Babylonia, 605-562 B.C. (2 Kings 24-25); but his son Belshazzar was the one warned of his coming downfall by handwriting on the wall (Daniel 5). a poet—Channing (see IV, 5).

6 Cato—*De Agricultura* (see I, 85).

7 Saturn—see VII, 15.

12 Vulcan—Roman god of fire. Terminus—Roman god of boundaries.

13 William Gilpin, 1724-1804—writer of picturesque travel works, including *Forest Scenery,* 1791 (from which the quotation is taken), and *The Highlands,* 1800, both of which Thoreau admired.

14 André Michaux, 1746-1802—French botanist and traveler, author of *Histoire des arbres forestiers de l'Amérique septentrionale,* 1810-13.

18 threads—a reference to Atropos, one of the Fates (see IV, 10).

19 "Never, bright flame . . ."—"The Wood-Fire," a poem published in the *Dial,* 1840, by Mrs. Ellen Sturgis Hooper, 1812-48.

14. Former Inhabitants; and Winter Visitors

When the weather turned snowy and Thoreau was deserted even by the hoot-owl, he had to conjure up former occupants of the woods for his only companions. One was a Negro slave Cato Ingraham, not Cato Uticensis but Concordiensis. Poor Cato was permitted to farm in Walden woods and planted walnuts for his old age, "but a younger and whiter speculator got them at last" (2). Another former inhabitant was a Negro woman named Zilpha, who made linen and muttered witch-like over a bubbling pot, "Ye are all bones, bones!" (3). Another slave, a handyman named Brister Freeman, lived down the road with his fortune-telling wife Fenda. Another former occupant named Breed made rum, which, Thoreau tells us sententiously, "first comes in the guise of a friend or hired man, and then robs and murders the whole family" (6). Breed's hut long survived its last owner until some mischievous boys set it afire a dozen years ago, occasioning an almost epic race of fire-fighting equipment and fire-fighters. Just one night after the fire, Thoreau, whose reading of Davenant's "Gondibert" in Chambers' collection of English poetry had been interrupted by the cries of "Fire!", walked past the smouldering ruins of the hut and discovered a lone survivor of the Breed family lamenting the destruction of the homestead. And there were other former inhabitants, including Wyman the potter, and, finally, an unusual Irishman named Hugh Quoil, called a colonel and rumored to have fought at Waterloo. He planted a little garden near Walden but was afflicted with such "terrible shaking fits" (11) that he did no hoeing, and later died. "Now only a dent in the earth marks the site of these dwellings, with buried cellar stones, and strawberries, raspberries, thimble-berries, hazel-berries, and sumachs growing in the sunny sward there . . ." (12). When old wells must be covered, wells of tears are often opened. After door, lintel, and sill are gone, "the vivacious lilac" flourishes, "unfolding its sweet-scented flowers each spring, to be plucked by the musing traveller . . ." (13). Thoreau wonders why Concord village has survived while no hamlet ever developed nearer Walden. "With such reminiscences I repeopled the woods and lulled myself asleep" (15). (1-15)

Almost entirely unvisited in winter, Thoreau recalled stories of the Great Snow of 1717, tramped through the deepening snow in "a meandering dotted line" (17) to keep an appointment with a beech and a birch, studied sleepy barrel owls, and unsuccessfully sought the tracks of rabbits and "the fine print, the small type, of a meadow mouse" (18) in the snow along the bitterly cold, wind-swept causeway of the railroad. Returning to his house, he would sometimes find evidence that the woodchopper had been there. Often he would "have a social 'crack'" with a certain "long-headed farmer" (19) who would crunch through the snow to him. Sometimes the poet would visit, for not even winter cold can deter a poet. Also a splendid friend, a philosopher, came to call. Thoreau praises this "true friend of man" most highly, concluding of him as follows: "A blue-robed man, whose fittest roof is the overarching sky which reflects his serenity. I do not see how he can ever die; Nature cannot spare him" (21). He and Thoreau—philosopher and hermit—often sat together and whittled their "shingles of thought well dried, . . . trying our knives, and admiring the clear yellowish grain of the pumpkin pine," and subjected the little Walden house to such conversational pressures that it "had to be calked with much dulness thereafter to stop the consequent leak" (22). One other village friend occasionally looked in on Thoreau, but the long-awaited Visitor never came.   (16-24)

NOTES

2   Cato Uticensis, 95-46 B.C.—Roman statesman and philosopher, great-grandson of Marcus Porcius Cato, author of *De Agricultura* (see I, 85).

4   Scipio Africanus, 237-183 B.C.—Roman general.

7   William D'Avenant, 1606-68—British poet laureate from 1638, author of the romantic epic *Gondibert,* 1651, reprinted in Alexander Chambers (1759-1834), ed., *Works of the English Poets,* 21 vols., 1810, which Thoreau read in full. The Nervii—a Gallo-Celtic tribe in the Netherlands area, defeated by Julius Caesar, 57 B.C.

10   potter's clay and wheel in Scripture—Jeremiah 18:3-6.

11   Reynard—the fox in innumerable beast fables.

12   "fate, free-will . . ."—Milton (see IV, 13), *Paradise Lost,* II.

20   a poet—Channing (see IV, 5).

21   another welcome visitor—Amos Bronson Alcott, 1799-1888, pedlar, teacher, visionary philosopher, father of Louisa May Alcott. "How blind that . . ."—Thomas Storer, 1571-1604, *The Life and Death of Thomas Wolsey Cardinall,* 1599. Old Mortality—Sir Walter Scott, 1771-1832, *Old Mortality,* 1816.

22   old settler—see V, 16, and IX, 11.

23   one other—Ralph Waldo Emerson, 1803-82.

24   Vishnu Purana—*The Vishnu Purana: A System of*

Hindu Mythology and Tradition, trans. H. H. Wilson (London, 1840). Vishnu—see II, 21. Purana—any one of the eighteen Sanskrit works called Puranas, which deal with the mythology and theology of creation, death, and rebirth.

15. Winter Animals

When the pond was solidly frozen, the whole neighborhood looked different and Thoreau enjoyed the strange views from the center of Walden. Even fishermen at a little distance looked unusual, like Eskimos, giants, or pygmies. The night sounds were forlorn but intriguing. The hoot owl's note was "the very *lingua vernacula* of Walden Wood." The honking of geese was startling until the cat owl harshly replied, "as if to expose and disgrace this intruder from Hudson's Bay by exhibiting a greater compass and volume of voice in a native" (2). The ice itself would whoop and crack—Thoreau's "great bedfellow in that part of Concord . . . [seemed] restless in its bed and would fain turn over, . . . troubled with flatulency and bad dreams" (3)—as would the ground too. (1-3)

Many animals and birds were well worth study. The foxes seemed to be laboring for light and trying to become dogs or even "rudimental, burrowing men" (4). Red squirrels would approach Thoreau's offerings of corn in a "trigonometrical way" and with "a ludicrous expression and a gratuitous somerset" (5). Jays screamed discordantly and then warily followed the squirrels for the corn they had dropped; but of jays Thoreau says, "They were manifestly thieves, and I had not much respect for them" (6). Chickadees also sought the dropped corn, "with faint flitting lisping notes, like the tinkling of icicles in the grass" (7). And partridges shirred through the branches, "jarring the snow from the dry leaves and twigs on high, which comes sifting down in the sunbeams like golden dust" (8). (4-8)

Next Thoreau writes in some detail about the foxes, which he has seen and about which old hunters have told him many stories. Thoreau dislikes the yelping packs of hounds, which seem "afflicted with a species of madness" as they pursue the fox. One hunter sought a hound of his which had been hunting by himself for a week; but the man was more curious about Thoreau than willing to listen to Thoreau's comments on the missing hound. "He had lost a dog, but found a man" (9), Thoreau sagely comments. Another hunter told of a wily fox which had eluded the violent hounds only to pause on a rock, his back to the nearby hunter, and listen, and be killed. The dogs rushed up at once but "were sobered into silence by the mystery" (10) of the dead fox. Still other hunters and also local written records informed Thoreau that some men once hunted bears near Walden, exchanging their skins for rum, and that they also once hunted moose, gray foxes, wild-cats, and deer. Thoreau concludes this section by noting that when he encountered hunting hounds at night in the woods, they would skulk out of his way as if afraid of him. (9-12)

Finally, Thoreau describes the wild mice's habit of gir-dling and thus killing pines by hungrily nibbling their bark in the famishing winter. He suggests that this process may be nature's way of thinning the often dense growth of pines. Then Thoreau describes the hares. One nested under his floor in the winter, startling him in the mornings by thumping her head. Hares ate his potato parings until he would open the door, when they would dash away "with a squeak and a bounce." They looked scrawny and fearful, "as if Nature no longer contained the breed of nobler bloods, but stood on her

last toes" (14), until the hares' magnificent speed proved that
nature still produced vigor and dignity. Thoreau closes by
remarking that every country needs rabbits and partridges,
"nearest allied to leaves and to the ground,—and to one another; it is either winged or it is legged" (15). They are as
natural as rustling leaves.   (13-15)

NOTES

9   Actaeon—a Greek hunter who innocently drank at the
pool of Artemis while she was bathing, for which she changed
him into a stag, and his own dogs pursued and killed him.

10   Weston Squire—possibly a pun on Squire Western in
Tom Jones, 1749, by Henry Fielding, 1707-54.

11   Nimrod—a hunter, from Genesis 10:8-9.

16. The Pond in Winter

Once when Thoreau awoke after a still winter sleep, he
fancied that he had been dreaming of difficult questions, such
as "what—how—when—where?" But when he looked out on
the dawn, he seemed to be urged forward into action and concluded that "Nature puts no question and answers none which
we mortals ask" (1). So he took axe and pail, and cut through
a foot of snow and then a foot of pond-ice for his water. Looking down into the perennially serene waters, in which the
pond's parlor was lighted "as through a window of ground
glass," Thoreau concluded that "Heaven is under our feet
as well as over our heads" (2).   (1-2)

The hardy fishermen come, linking the wintry little towns
together. These men have as much natural lore as the towns-

people have artificial, and they fish most skillfully. Next Thoreau extols the beauties of Walden pickerel, "fabulous fishes," "the animalized *nuclei* or crystals of the Walden water," "themselves small Waldens in the animal kingdom, Waldenses." And when caught they die easily, "with a few convulsive quirks . . . giv[ing] up their watery ghosts, like a mortal translated before his time to the thin air of heaven" (5). (3-5)

Thoreau was once anxious to sound the depths of supposedly bottomless Walden. "It is remarkable [he says] how long men will believe in the bottomlessness of a pond without taking the trouble to sound it" (6). He found Walden Pond to be 102 feet deep and so regular that he could estimate different depths along the line across the greatest width. The pond and others similar to it are relatively shallow, compared to their surface dimensions, and therefore are like plates and not at all like cups between the hills. Thoreau also studied bars across several coves at Walden. To test his skill in water surveying, he estimated the point of greatest depth of 41-acre White Pond, missing it, as he later verified, by only a hundred feet. Thoreau concludes that we could make wonderfully refined calculations concerning natural phenomena if we only had more than our present few natural laws to work with. Then he applies his pond laws to the ethics of a particular hypothetical man: "Perhaps we need only to know how his shores trend and his adjacent country or circumstances, to infer his depth and concealed bottom. . . . It is true, we are such poor navigators that our thoughts, for the most part, stand off and on upon a harborless coast, are conversant only with the bights of the bays of poesy, or steer for the public ports of entry, and go into the dry docks of science, where they merely refit for this world, and no natural currents concur to individualize them" (13). (6-13)

Thoreau could not discover an inlet or an outlet for Walden, although he was shown by some workmen that ice from one part of the pond was thinner than ice from another part, which suggested the presence of a warm inlet near the thinner ice. He also observed an undulation of the ice, even when it was sixteen inches thick. "Who knows [he wonders] but if our instruments were delicate enough we might detect an undulation in the crust of the earth?" (15). And he noted the manner in which water ran into holes cut in the ice, floating the nearby still-solid mass, and the way the holes froze and when followed by rain produced web-like and rosette-like formations. (14-15)

Thoreau was amused by the diligent workmen who farmed the topsoil of Walden for their crop of ice in the winter of 1846-47. They did it for a gentleman farmer who wanted to double his fortune, which was already a half-million dollars. Thoreau was partly pleased when one worker fell through the ice and had to thaw out at his nearby house, and pleased also when Walden's "frozen soil took a piece of steel out of a plowshare" (17). He describes the men's procedure of cutting ice cakes, sledding them ashore, stacking them with horse-worked blocks and tackles, and insulating the monstrous pile with hay against the eating wind. The resulting "hoary ruin, built of azure-tinted marble," looked like "the abode of winter, that old man we see in the almanac" (18). Curiously, this huge heap of ice, weighing an estimated ten thousand tons, never got to market, but stayed in the same spot until it had all melted two Septembers later. Thoreau wonders at the color of Walden ice, green close up but blue from a distance. When a cake slips from an ice-man's sled into the village street, it "lies there for a week like a great emerald." He remarks on the everlasting sweetness of ice compared to a bucket of water, which quickly turns putrid: "It is commonly said that this is the difference between the affections and the intellect" (19). Thoreau sits at his hut window, watches a hundred Irishmen plowing up the pond ice, and thinks comfortably that in thirty days "the pure sea-green Walden water there . . . [will be] reflecting the clouds and the trees, and sending up its evaporations in solitude, and no traces will appear that a man has ever stood there" (20). (16-20)

Sweltering people throughout the world—from Charleston to Bombay—may use Walden ice, but, says Thoreau, "I bathe my intellect in the stupendous and cosmogonal philosophy of the Bhagvat-Geeta . . . I lay down the book and go to my well for water, and lo! there I meet the servant of the Bramin . . . The pure Walden water is mingled with the sacred water of the Ganges" (21).

NOTES

5 Waldenses—members of a 12th-century Protestant sect in southern France.

6 Styx—see IV, 21.

7 Gilpin—*The Highlands* (see XIII, 13). "So high as . . ."—Milton, *Paradise Lost,* VII (see IV, 13).

17 Hyperborean—pertaining to Greek mythological people living beyond the north wind. Tartarus—Greek mythological abyss below Hades.

18 Valhalla—see X, 1.

21 Bhagvat-Geeta—see I, 79. Bramin—Brahman, a member of the first Hindu caste of India. Brahma—see II, 21. Vishnu—see II, 21. Indra—see V, 11. Vedas—see II, 14. Atlantis—mythical submerged island in the Atlantic Ocean. Hesperides—Greek mythological maidens who guarded the golden apples which grow in their western or Hyperborean

island or coastal garden. Hanno—see I, 33. Ternate and Tidore
—Dutch East Indian spice islands. Alexander, 356-328 B.C.—
conqueror of the then known world.

17. *Spring*

Being deeper and having no stream running through it,
Walden breaks up later than other ponds nearby, usually
starting to do so about the first of April. The sun begins to
work on the ice both by warming the air above and by pene-
trating the ice and thus warming the water beneath it. Then
the ice begins to rot or "comb" (1)—that is, look like a honey-
comb. Each day epitomizes a year, with the morning resem-
bling the spring, noon summer, and so on. In the morning, the
booming ice stretches itself, like a man rousing himself after
sleep; it takes a noon siesta, and so on, often booming again
at night. Thoreau wonders that so large, cold, and thick-
skinned a creature as Walden should be so sensitive, and yet
it is. (1-2)

Spring coming to the pond was the greatest of spectacles
for Thoreau. The ice begins to rot, birds and animals become
aware of the nearness of spring, and suddenly after a single
warm rain the ice all goes. An old hunter once told Thoreau
that he mistook the grinding of thawing and drifting ice for
the sudden rush of many birds. Next the sun and warm winds
melt the banks of snow, and they run off into rivulets "whose
veins are filled with the blood of winter" (5). Especially intriguing and suggestive to Thoreau was the flowing of sand
and clay during spring thaws. The phenomenon was best observed down the sides of a railroad cut. The sand would erupt

like lava, and the streams would "overlap and interlace" until
they resembled inanimate currents less than vegetation, for
example "the laciniated, lobed, and imbricated thalluses of
some lichens . . . or . . . coral, . . . leopards' paws or birds'
feet, . . . brains or lungs or bowels, and excrements of all
kinds" (6). Thoreau sees this sandy clay as "the laboratory of
the Artist who made the world and men," and he theorizes
that this almost living flow is "an [evolutionary] anticipation
of the vegetable leaf," further that "feathers and wings of
birds are still drier and thinner leaves," that "ice begins with
crystal leaves," and that a "tree . . . is but one leaf, and rivers
are still vaster leaves" (7). Returning to more details of the
flowing sandy clay, Thoreau suggests that in its sentient mo-
tion and progress it is almost living, its silicious matter like a
bone system, and its soil and organic matter like cellular tis-
sue. "What is man but a mass of thawing clay?" (8), he concludes extravagantly. (3-8)

    "Thus it seemed that this one hillside illustrated the prin-
ciple of all the operations of Nature. The Maker of this earth
but patented a leaf" (9). With this statement as a transition,
Thoreau now turns to his description of the coming of spring.
The emergence of the frost—"like a dormant quadruped from
its burrow" (10)—"precedes the green and flowery spring, as
mythology precedes regular poetry." All the earth comes to life
again—"not a fossil earth, but a living earth; compared with
whose great central life all animal and vegetable life is merely
parasitic" (9). Very early vegetation, tender and fragile, springs
up after a few warm and dry days, as though Winter, not rude
and boisterous after all, were lover-like adorning Summer.
Then red squirrels return with their "vocal pirouetting and
gurgling sounds" (12), and then the first sparrow, then blue-
birds and red-wings and marsh hawks. And finally "The grass
flames up on the hillsides like a spring fire . . . not yellow

but green . . . the symbol of perpetual youth . . . lifting its
spear of last year's hay with the fresh life below" (13). Walden melts and reveals "the bare face of the pond full of glee
and youth . . . Walden was dead and is alive again" (14).
A proof of spring is a sudden miraculous influx of summer
skies. Then pine and oak begin to brighten and appear alive
again; geese, ducks, and pigeons fly back; the tortoise and the
frog herald the new season; and vernal plants and winds
spring up. ˙ (9-17)

Thoreau now suggests that each new season "seems best
to us in its turn" (18); yet it is the rains of spring which
deepen the green shades of nature, and the mornings of spring
in which "all men's sins are forgiven" (19), even those of our
thieving, drunken, sensual neighbor, whom in spring we must
pardon because spring is God's pardon to us all. (18-21)

On April 29, while fishing, Thoreau saw a graceful, tumbling, happy hawk flashing its wings high above. "It was the
most ethereal flight I have ever witnessed. It did not simply
flutter like a butterfly, nor soar like the larger hawks, but it
sported with proud reliance in the fields of air; mounting
again and again with its strange chuckle, it repeated its free
and beautiful fall, turning over and over like a kite, and then
recovering from its lofty tumbling, as if it had never set its
foot on *terra firma*. It appeared to have no companion in the
universe,—sporting there alone,—and to need none but the
morning and the ether with which it played" (22). In addition
to this windfall, Thoreau caught some fine "silver and bright
cupreous fishes" and also bathed in the pure light of spring.
"There needs no stronger proof of immortality. All things
must live in such a light" (23), Thoreau goes on ecstatically.
Village life would atrophy if it were not for unexplored nature
surrounding it. Curiously, we want to explore this nature even
while we want it to continue unexplorable. The inexhaustible

vigor of nature, its titanic strength, its vastness, and even its gruesome and deadly processes all combine to tell us about its "inviolable health" (24). (22-24)

In conclusion here, Thoreau reports that in May various trees began to leaf out and various birds to sing. Pollen filled the air. And the loon reappeared in the pond. "And so the seasons went rolling on into summer, as one rambles into higher and higher grass" (25). Thus went Thoreau's first year at Walden, with the second similar to it. Finally he left the pond on September 6, 1847. (25-26)

NOTES

9 Jean François Champollion, 1790-1832—French historian, hieroglyphist, and founder of Egyptology. hands of the potter—see XIV, 10.

10 Thor—Norse war and thunder god.

13 "et primitus oritur . . ."—Varro (see VII, 15).

18 "Eurus ad Auroram . . ."—Ovid, 43 B.C.-18 A.D., *Metamorphoses,* I.

20-21 "A return to goodness . . ."—*Works of Mencius* (see XI, 11). "The Golden Age . . ."—Ovid, *Metamorphoses,* I (see 18 above).

23 "O Death, where . . ."—1 Corinthians 15:55.

25 Calidas—Kalidas, fl. c. 5th century, Hindu dramatist and lyric poet, *Sakuntala,* V.

18. Conclusion

Doctors wisely recommend a change of scene for patients, and yet much travel is foolish. "One hastens to southern Africa to chase the giraffe; but surely that is not the game he would be after. How long, pray, would a man hunt giraffes if he could?" Further, "It is not worth the while to go round the world to count the cats in Zanzibar." Instead, it is surely better to hunt oneself. "Be . . . the Mungo Park, the Lewis and Clark and Frobisher, of your own streams and oceans; explore your own higher latitudes . . . there are continents and seas in the moral world to which every man is an isthmus or an inlet, yet unexplored by him . . . it is easier to sail many thousand miles through cold and storm and cannibals, in a government ship, with five hundred men and boys to assist one, than it is to explore the private sea, the Atlantic and Pacific Ocean of one's being alone" (2).   (1-2)

Mirabeau became a highway robber to learn the degree of resolution necessary to place oneself in opposition to social laws. But, Thoreau comments, while this was manly it was also foolish, because the sane man finds himself sufficiently in opposition to society by obeying more sacred personal laws. (3)

Next, Thoreau explains that he left the woods because he had more lives to live and could spare no more time for his Walden experiment. Also he dislikes falling into a routine and noted with regret that he had quickly worn a path from his door to the pond. He wants to follow no "ruts of tradition and conformity" (4).

From his experiment he learned that "if one advances confidently in the direction of his dreams, and endeavors to live the life which he has imagined, he will meet with a success unexpected in common hours" (5). And if one simplifies his life, univeral laws become less complex, solitude becomes no solitude at all, nor is poverty poor, or weakness weak. Go ahead and build castles in the air, but then be sure to place the foundations beneath them.   (5)

Far from lamenting his occasional extravagance of speech, Thoreau now says that it is his fear that his "expression may not be *extra-vagant* enough, may not wander far enough beyond the narrow limits of [his] daily experience" (6). He does not want to concern himself merely with dull perceptions and common sense, but would actually prefer to be called obscure: after all, pure Walden's blue ice is criticized by some customers, who prefer the weedy-tasting white ice of Cambridge. Further, some critics of America and modern times say that now there are only intellectual dwarfs compared to ancient and even Elizabethan giants. To this Thoreau would answer, "A living dog is better than a dead lion" (9); let us mind our own business and be what we are. Yet we should not all be desperately anxious to succeed in desperate businesses. "If a man does not keep pace with his companions, perhaps it is because he hears a different drummer. Let him step to the music which he hears, however measured or far away" (10). Then Thoreau tells a parable of the artist of Kouroo who wanted to make a perfect staff. He carefully chose his stock, slowly peeled it, delicately smoothed and polished it, and painstakingly attached ferrule and gem-studded head. While he worked, whole dynasties and even constellations changed, but he remained perennially youthful. When he finished his staff, "it suddenly expanded before the eyes of the astonished artist into the fairest of all the creations of Brahma" (11). How could it be anything but wonderful? Thoreau concludes, since the material and the art were pure. (6-11)

Be true, squarely face your life—no matter how mean—and live it contentedly. Be cheerful, independent, and gratefully poor and humble. Pay little attention to new things. Instead, "Turn the old; return to them." Avoid dissipating your talents in response to a multitude of influences. Remember that

"Money is not required to buy one necessary of the soul" (13). Avoid "all transient and fleeting phenomena" but instead "gravitate toward that which most strongly and rightfully attracts . . . There is a solid bottom everywhere." Instead of nailing into plaster and lath, "feel for the furring" and "Drive a nail home and clinch it so faithfully that you can wake up in the night and think of your work with satisfaction" (14). Again Thoreau comes out in support of truth: "Rather than love, than money, than fame, give me truth." He would far rather be lightly fed by a sincere and truthful host than richly wined and dined at an "inhospitable board" (15). He would rather visit a man housed in a hollow tree but with regal manners than call on a cold king in his palace. (12-15)

And now Thoreau concludes his book. He tells us that too often we pride ourselves on the past and on the accomplishments of others. Meanwhile we remain unaware of our own potentialities, and contentedly side with the ordinary and the mean. Instead, we should realize that each of us has a tide within him which could float an empire like a chip. "The life in us is like the water in the river. It may rise this year higher than man has ever known it, and flood the parched uplands." Remember the recent story of a beautiful and hardy bug which had been buried for sixty years in a kitchen table made of apple-wood. It came out one day, "hatched perchance by the heat of an urn." Thoreau finds his faith in resurrection and immortality greatly strengthened by this event. "Who knows [he continues] what beautiful and winged life . . . may unexpectedly come forth from amidst society's most trivial . . . furniture, to enjoy its perfect summer life at last!" (18). Not everyone will realize this, Thoreau warns. Mere time will not bring the real dawn to all. "Only that day dawns to which we are awake. There is more day to dawn. The sun is but a morning star" (19).

NOTES

1 Tierra del Fuego—see I, 17.

2 "Direct your eye . . ."—William Habington, 1605-54, "To My Honoured Friend Sir Ed. P. Knight," 1635. Sir John Franklin, 1786-1847—British naval officer and Arctic explorer lost seeking the Northwest Passage; in the 1850's his wife organized attempts to find evidence of his last whereabouts, which evidence was found in 1859. Henry Grinnell, 1799-1874, an American, financed Elisha Kent Kane's unsuccessful 1850 and 1853 expeditions in search of Franklin. Mungo Park, 1771-1806—Scottish explorer of Africa who drowned in the Niger River. Meriwether Lewis, 1774-1809, and William Clark, 1770-1838—co-commanded the Lewis and Clark Expedition 1803-6 to find a land route from Illinois to the Pacific Ocean. Sir Martin Frobisher, 1535?-94—English mariner and explorer. "Errat, et extremos alter . . ."—Claudian, d. 408?—Latin epic poet, "Old Man of Verona." Symmes' Hole—John Cleves Symmes, 1780-1829, advanced the theory that the earth was hollow and open at both poles, especially in *Symmes's Theory of Concentric Spheres; Demonstrating that the Earth Is Hollow, Habitable Within, and Widely Open about the Poles,* Cincinnati, 1826. Sphinx—when Oedipus in Sophocles's *Oedipus* answers her riddle, the monstrous Sphinx kills herself.

3 Comte de Mirabeau, 1749-91—French Revolutionary leader.

6 Bright—common 19th-century name for an ox.

7 "They pretend . . ."—Garcin de Tassy, 1794-1878, *Histoire de la Littérature Hindoui,* 1839.

11 "There was an artist . . ."—leading Thoreau scholars suggest that Thoreau made up this beautiful fable as an allegory of his own life and ideals. Kalpa—a Hindu period of vast time, rather than a star. Brahma—see II, 21.

13 "The philosopher said . . ."—Confucius, *Analects* (see I, 15). "and lo! creation . . ."—Joseph Blanco White, 1775-1841, "Night and Death" (a sonnet uniquely praised by S. T. Coleridge), 1828. Croesus—immensely wealthy 6th-century B.C. Lydian king.

14 *tintinnabulum*—see VII, 6. Mameluke bey—a Mameluke prisoner of the Egyptian Pasha in 1811 escaped a general massacre in Cairo by leaping his horse from a fortress wall to the ground (Mameluke, a member of the military caste dominating Egypt 1254-1811; bey, a Turkish title of respect). Webster—see XII, 14. kittly-benders—children's game of running on dangerously thin ice without breaking through it.

19 John—a familiar name for a representative Britisher. Jonathan—a familiar name for a representative American.

ARTISTRY IN *WALDEN*

Thoreau was a skillful mason (XIII, 5*), and he was a careful handler of words. In *Walden,* his individual words were his bricks, his building blocks. He put them together into course-like sentences, his sentences into wall-like paragraphs, his paragraphs into well-built chapters, and finally his eighteen chapter-houses into a well-planned city—or, as he might express it, into a rural *com-munity* (VI, 17).

If we begin with the simplest structural unit in *Walden* and consider the diction, we are quickly impressed. Thoreau's vocabulary is striking. It includes simple and homely words graphically used. For example, Thoreau writes as follows: "I went to the woods because I wished to live deliberately, to front only the essential facts of life, and see if I could not learn what it had to teach, and not, when I came to die, discover that I had not lived" (II, 16). In those forty-four words, only five are of more than one syllable each. They are *because, deliberately, only, essential,* and *discover.* They are all basic enough to be understood by a ten-year-old. Two, *deliberately* and *essential,* are placed with special care, to force the reader to slow down and respond to the intended emphasis. Although Thoreau does not italicize the words *deliberately* and *essential,* if we read the sentence aloud we will undoubtedly stress them and especially the *lib* and *sen* syllables. Thoreau tells us to "Simplify, simplify" (II, 17), and he certainly uses simple diction much of the time in *Walden.*

* Parenthetical Roman references are to chapters in *Walden;* Arabic, to paragraphs.

But plenty of harder words, usually with Greek and Latin roots, appear in *Walden*, sometimes with their roots half exposed. For example, we find *aliment, caryatides, cerulean, cynosure, deliquium, diluvian, dishabille, ebriosity, exogenous, exuviae, flatulency, fluviatile, foliaceous, glaucous, handselled, internecine, periplus, piscine, plectrum, praetors, potamogetons, sinecure,* and *vulpine.* Occasionally Thoreau calls attention to the root of the word, as when he boasts that he wants his literary expression to be *extra-vagant* (XVIII, 6) and when he criticizes professors for merely professing (I, 9). Often he uses relatively common words in unusual or even original forms, or coins his own words, as in *auroral, cerealian, Concordiensis, excrementitious, manurance, rudimental, silicious, spectatordom,* and *noveldom.* He is fond of oddly compounded words, for example *low-lived, sound-conditioned, last-uttered, night-walked, self-emancipation, hundred-gated, Make-a-stir, star-veiled, men-harriers,* and *once-and-a-half-witted.* His vocabulary is swelled both by homely and by scientific words and phrases which as an amateur scientist he would naturally know: *Aldebaran, Altair, cerasus pumila, chivin, hardhack, imbricated, johnswort, laciniated, lenticular, mavis, pinnate, Portulaca oleracea, Rhus glabra,* and *succedaneous.* And his vocabulary is augmented by numerous literary, philosophical, and historical allusions, from Juno, Jupiter, and Hercules, through Homer and Virgil, to the Hindu sacred writings and Confucius, down to modern times in England and New England. In short, Thoreau is in the tradition of those nervously alive "baroque" stylists from Sir Francis Bacon and Robert Burton and Sir Thomas Browne through to Herman Melville and Emily Dickinson and on down to Gerard Manley Hopkins, James Joyce, and William Faulkner.

One proof of Thoreau's awareness of language is his delight in puns, of which there are dozens in *Walden.* Thus, in the midst of his deadly serious explanation of why he went to Walden we have a charming pun: "I did not wish to live what was not life, living is so dear . . ." (II, 16), *dear* meaning both "expensive" and "precious." The following are a few other examples among his many puns. "For a long time, I was reporter to a journal, of no very wide circulation" (I, 27), *journal* really meaning only "diary" here. "Did you ever think what those sleepers are that underlie the railroad? Each one is a man . . . They are sound sleepers" (II, 17), *sleepers* also meaning "railroad ties." Timber is shipped by the railroads to manufacturing towns with "huge and lumbering civility," while carloads of torn sails so eloquently tell of storms at sea that they are "proof-sheets which need no correction" (IV, 7, 12). "My 'best' room, however, my withdrawing room, always ready for company, . . . was the pine wood behind my house" (VI, 4), the pun being on *drawing room*. A certain fisherman "belonged to the ancient sect of Coenobites [Cenobites]" (IX, 2), the word *Cenobites* meaning members of a religious community, being pronounced "see no bites." Walden pickerel are "small Waldens . . . , Waldenses" (XVI, 5), *Waldenses* also being members of a twelfth-century Protestant sect in southern France. And in the spring, nature "turn[s] over a new leaf," "Thaw with his gentle persuasion is more powerful than Thor . . . ," and formerly "widowed Nature wears" "decent weeds" (XVII, 9, 10, 11).

Allied to puns are figures of speech. Thoreau is unusually fond of similes and metaphors, extended personifications and imaginative analogies. Ordinarily his images are brief and graphic, with certain key words extensively used—words such as *clothes, egg, eye, gem, leaf, roof, seed, star, wave,* and *wing.* More rarely the image may spread over several sentences. The chapters with the greatest concentration of images are "Sounds" (IV), "The Village" (VIII), "Baker Farm" (X), "Spring"

(XVII), and "Conclusion" (XVIII). Those with the fewest images are "Economy" (I), "Visitors" (VI), and "Higher Laws" (XI). In general, Thoreau is inspired to figurative flights by aspects of nature and his responses to them; mundane matters like money and townspeople who visit him deaden his trope-making faculty. "Economy" and "Visitors" have far fewer than half the number of images per page that "Sounds" and "Spring" have.

The biggest single category of metaphors and similes in *Walden* concerns nature. Thoreau graphically compares people, processes, and ideas to animals, birds, fish, flowers, fruits, insects, plants, stars, and water. Here are some examples. He satirically says that the village contains "busy men, as curious to me as if they had been prairie dogs, each sitting at the mouth of its burrow, or running over to a neighbor's to gossip" (VIII, 1). Thoreau explains that his purpose in writing *Walden* is not to compose "an ode to dejection, but to brag as lustily as chanticleer in the morning, standing on his roost, if only to wake my neighbors up" (II, 7). He and his revered philosophical visitor wade together conversationally with such gentleness that "the fishes of thought were not scared from the stream, nor feared any angler on the bank, but came and went grandly" (XIV, 22). One pervasive Thoreauvian moral certainly is that "If the day and the night are such that you greet them with joy, and life emits a fragrance like flowers and sweet-scented herbs, is more elastic, more starry, more immortal,—that is your success" (XI, 7). But most people are so coarsened by the labors of life that "its finer fruits cannot be plucked by them. Their fingers, from excessive toil, are too clumsy and tremble too much for that" (I, 6). To Thoreau, college dormitories are "crowded hives" (V, 12), while noisily marching soldiers produce a "hum as if somebody's bees had swarmed" (VII, 6). But the happy hermit, in his bean-field and at twilight, "grew in those seasons like the corn in the night" (IV, 2), while "The true harvest of [his] daily life" was "intangible and indescribable as the tints of morning or evening . . . a little star dust caught, a segment of the rainbow . . . clutched" (XI, 7). Finally, during one delicious evening Thoreau feels marvelously attuned to everything in nature, and we read: "Sympathy with the fluttering alder and poplar leaves almost takes my breath; yet, like the lake, my serenity is rippled, but not ruffled" (V, 1).

The next largest class of images concerns classical mythology and literature. Thoreau makes comparisons involving such elements of Greek and Roman legends as Actaeon, Aesculapius, Antaeus, Atropos, Aurora, Atlas, Ceres, fauns, Hercules, Hygeia, Juno, Jupiter, Olympus, Orpheus, Minerva, Saturn, satyrs, sibyls, Tartarus, Terminus, vestal fire, Vulcan, and wood-nymphs. Homer's *Iliad* and *Odyssey* figure in more imagery than any other literary works. Hindu scriptures are often quoted, but Thoreau typically makes literal rather than figurative use of this body of writing. It is surprising that the Bible does almost nothing for Thoreau's imagery; perhaps in the following unique Biblical figure is buried his reason: ". . . I encountered many a blustering and nipping wind . . . ; and when the frost had smitten me on one cheek, heathen as I was, I turned to it the other cheek" (XIV, 18). It should be added, of course, that Thoreau frequently adapts Biblical phraseology and integrates it into his own prose.

Although Thoreau could describe his landscapes with a true painter's eye, he employs very few pictorial images. He has hardly more sculpture figures, and they are always routine ones. Drama was a lost art for Thoreau, if his imagery is any guide. And music provides little more inspiration, although he played the flute and did seemingly hear the music of the spheres while at his beloved pond. The sound of church bells wafted to him from nearby towns "acquires a certain vibratory hum, as if the pine needles in the horizon were the strings of a harp which it swept" (IV, 15); and "Many an irksome noise, go a long way off, is heard as music, a proud sweet satire on the meanness of our lives" (XI, 10).

Of the several minor categories of images—clothes, food, houses, sailing, religion, science, and war—perhaps only clothes, houses, and religion are of interest here. It is understandable that Thoreau, who made such forthright comments on clothing, might fashion a few strange metaphors out of stitches, seams, coats, skirts, and the like. Almost at the outset, he tells his readers to adapt to themselves such portions of his book as they wish—"I trust that none will stretch the seams in putting on the coat, for it may do good service to him whom it fits" (I, 2). During the sunrise, Thoreau watches the pond "throwing off its nightly clothing of mist" (II, 10). In winter it grows its own coat—of ice—"a thick new garment" (XVII, 1). The high-circling night-hawk screams "as if the heavens were rent, torn at last to very rags and tatters, and yet a seamless cope remained" (VII, 5). And the miraculous advent of spring convinces the poet that "Earth is still in her swaddling-clothes, and stretches forth baby fingers on every side" (XVII, 9).

Naturally an adept house-builder like Thoreau would occasionally wedge carpentry figures into his book. Thus we read of "the various mansions of the universe" (I, 13), the "icy shutter over [Walden's] broad skylight" (IX, 21), "the very abutment of a rainbow's arch" (X, 2), "shingles of thought well dried" (XIV, 22), and the "unroof[ed] . . . house of fishes" (XVI, 16).

The religion imagery is surprisingly poor: we have nothing of significance deriving from Old or New Testament thought, only a few routine figures involving angels, choirs, ghosts, incense, pagodas, and vicars, and perhaps as a sufficient explanation simply this from pantheistic Thoreau: "Sometimes I rambled to pine groves, standing like temples. . . . These were the shrines I visited both summer and winter" (X, 1).

In addition to patterns of figures involving birds and beasts and bugs, classical reading, and so on, a small number of tropes and symbolically employed objects coalesce into motifs of circularity—egg, ring, berry, eye, well, pond, horizon, ocean, cyclical nature, globe, moon, sun, and star—while still others, fewer in number but of great importance, provide challenging patterns of death and rebirth and renewal, and of farewell, travel, and return.

The next compositional unit for study in Thoreau is the sentence. *Walden* is a rhetorician's source-book, containing as it does sentences of almost every conceivable type. Some are very brief: "It needs no fence" (IX, 18), "His manners were truly regal" (XVIII, 15), "Hither the clean wild ducks come" (IX, 34), and the like. Others are infinitely more complex. If Thoreau wishes to describe an action made up of several simultaneously occurring parts, he usually does so in one vast sentence. Thus—

> When I meet the engine with its train of cars moving off with planetary motion,—or, rather, like a comet, for the beholder knows not if with that velocity and with that direction it will ever revisit this system, since its orbit does not look like a returning curve,—with its steam cloud like a banner streaming behind in golden and silver wreaths, like many a downy cloud which I have seen, high in the heavens, unfolding its masses to the light,—as if this travelling demigod, this cloud-compeller, would ere long take the sunset sky for the livery of his train; when I hear the iron horse make the hills

echo with his snort like thunder, shaking the earth with
his feet, and breathing fire and smoke from his nostrils
(what kind of winged horse or fiery dragon they will
put into the new Mythology I don't know), it seems as
if the earth had got a race now worthy to inhabit it.
(IV, 8)

The full dozen clauses of that sentence may be hooked together like the train which it describes, but it also moves like
a well-powered train and it gets a load of meanings to their
destination. Similar in length and sinuosity is the seven-clause,
nine-participle sentence in which Thoreau beautifully describes
the trigonometrical progress of the frisky, nibbling, listening,
thinking red squirrel (XV, 5). A much longer sentence is the
one which splendidly summarizes Thoreau's dream of an ideal
house, of substantial materials and functional design, of one
cavernous room in which the weary wanderer may come to
wash and eat and talk and rest, and in which all simple necessities will be conveniently located (XIII, 7).

Thoreau also effectively strings short sentences together.
For example, of the following six consecutive sentences, describing partridges, five are simple and only one is complex.

The remarkably adult yet innocent expression of their
open and serene eyes is very memorable. All intelligence
seems reflected in them. They suggest not merely the
purity of infancy, but a wisdom clarified by experience.
Such an eye was not born when the bird was, but is
coeval with the sky it reflects. The woods do not yield
another such a gem. The traveller does not often look
into such a limpid well.   (XII, 10)

For another example, notice the hammer-like terseness of the
following didactic sentences from "Conclusion":

Cultivate poverty like a garden herb, like sage. Do not
trouble yourself much to get new things, whether clothes
or friends. Turn the old; return to them. Things do not
change; we change. Sell your clothes and keep your
thoughts. God will see that you do not want society.
(XVIII, 13)

More important than length of sentences are both emphasis and thought movement. The stress of a typical Thoreauvian
sentence falls naturally where it belongs. This is so because
Thoreau the lecturer got into the habit of directly addressing
his reader, as though he were pointing a finger between his
eyes. Any alert reader of *Walden* can find a hundred examples
of such sentences in no time. Here are three. "No wonder that
Alexander carried the Iliad with him on his expeditions in a
precious casket" (III, 5). There are four stresses here, light
ones on *Alexander* and *Iliad,* a heavier one on *precious,* and a
very heavy one on the terminal *casket.* A dupal rhythm exists
in the following sentence, which crests at *books,* then subsides
to *summer,* to rise again at *hoed beans*: "I did not read books
the first summer; I hoed beans" (IV, 2). Finally, notice the
more intricate rhythm—almost a waltz and a slide—in the
following sentence: "The stove not only [1] took up room and
[2] scented the house, but it [3] concealed the fire, and
[slide] I felt as if I had lost a companion" (XIII, 19). Far
more complicated patterns of emphasis and gliding exist in
Thoreau's longer sentences.

More often than not a given sentence addresses itself to a
topic which the next sentence carries forward in a wave effect.
Read, for example, the 22-sentence paragraph (I, 73) in which
Thoreau compares his studious life at the pond with the expensive but only theoretical education of the Cambridge student. He begins by boasting that he built a shelter at a cost

no greater than a scholar's annual rent. If he brags, it is for humanity. No, he boasts personally too but is only speaking the truth. The college student's quarters are small, inconvenient, noisy, costly, and inefficiently built and managed. While tuition is high, the most educative part of college life is the free associations with fellow-students. The method of building a college is deplorable: others lay the foundation, while the potential students fit themselves for the coming institution. But the students should lay the foundation and not shirk their responsibilities in order to gain undeserved leisure. Students should use their heads, yes; but they should also live fully, not merely play at life or study it. We learn by living. Should a young man learn surveying, for example, by studying under a professor or by surveying nature with his own eyes? If a boy should dig ore, smelt it, and make a knife, would he not have gained more than one who attended lectures on metallurgy and was then given a knife by his father? A turn down the harbor teaches more of navigation than a college class does. We study political economy in school, but not the economy of living. Therefore, while reading Adam Smith in college, the young scholar runs his father into debt. Thus Thoreau begins his paragraph by boasting of his economy and ends by deploring the lack of it in other so-called students. The whole paragraph walks along, with regular signposts such as *thus, for instance, better than this* . . . , *I mean, this,* and *The consequence is* . . . guiding the follower. In addition, key words like *shelter, boast, truth, student, foundations, life, course,* and *economy* make clear the goal of the walk.

But other paragraphs do not move so straight or handle the reader so gently. Sometimes Thoreau begins a paragraph arm-in-arm with his gentle reader, so to speak, but ends it by facing that astonished person around, snarling at him, and then leaving him abashed and speechless. Consider the last paragraph of "The Ponds" (IX, 34). It begins as follows: "White Pond and Walden are great crystals on the surface of the earth, Lakes of Light." We nod in agreement, because Thoreau has long been poetically describing these two favorite spots of his. Then he adds that if they were congealed and small, men would treat the two ponds like the gems they really are. Again we agree. Next he chides us all and includes himself—"we disregard them, and run after the diamond of Kohinoor." But by this time he has withdrawn his arm from ours and has separated himself from us. Thoreau has assuredly sought no wealth. When he adds that "Nature has no human inhabitant who appreciates her," the candid among us would surely except Thoreau himself from his almost universal de-nunciation. Then he goes on, "what youth or maiden conspires with the wild luxuriant beauty of Nature?" We name Tho-reau as such a youth, certainly, and rush to read the end. "She flourishes almost alone, far from the towns where they [Tho-reau does not say 'we'] reside. Talk of heaven! ye [not 'we'] disgrace earth." And Thoreau leaves us ashamed and alone: "we" has subtly become "ye"; nature is far from our residence; and Thoreau says nothing more in that paragraph, or that chapter.

Such about-face paragraphs are numerous in *Walden* and are perhaps more typical, as they are certainly more significant and provocative, than the linear paragraphs which urge us to accompany the author on the straight path of his reasoning.

It is notable that Thoreau varies his paragraph lengths as he does his sentence lengths. Some paragraphs are very short, for example the following, quoted in full: "Once more, on the left, where are seen the wall and lilac bushes by the wall, in the now open field, lived Nutting and Le Grosse. But to re-turn toward Lincoln" (XIV, 9). This type of paragraph has the effect of giving the attentive reader one more glance from an angle of the road before Thoreau moves him along in a different direction. On the other hand, the last paragraph of "Reading" (III, 12), which contains astute criticism of nineteenth-century materialism, is a spacious one of thirty sentences because Thoreau needs room in which to turn around and lash about. Similarly, he loads his paragraphs detailing the multitudinous cargo of trains (IV, 12, 13) precisely in order to weary us and make us gratefully turn with him to the solitude of nature. The next paragraph begins, "Now that the cars are gone by and all the restless world with them, and the fishes in the pond no longer feel their rumbling, I am more alone than ever" (14).

Almost everything that has been remarked concerning Thoreau's sentences and paragraphs can be said of his individual chapters. "The Village" (VIII) is deliberately short, almost insultingly so, as though Thoreau wants us to know that he has little to say on this dull subject. In addition, the chapter is filled with explicit criticism of the tawdriness of village life. Also, the movement of this brief chapter is an arc, even a circle: Thoreau enjoys sauntering to the village largely because he can quickly turn around and launch himself home again to the pond. On the other hand, "The Ponds" (IX) is the longest chapter, aside from "Economy" (I), which is unique through being introductory and explanatory. "The Ponds" takes us disarmingly by the elbow on a tour around, on, into, and beyond Walden Pond, only to rebuke us at the end, as we have seen, with "Talk of heaven! ye disgrace earth" (IX, 34). The movement of "The Ponds" thus is partially that of a spiral, with Thoreau splitting off from our dead-end track and making his way alone and silent back to his hut.

At least twice, Thoreau moves not geographically but temporally. In "Former Inhabitants; and Winter Visitors"

(XIV) he places himself firmly and cozily in wintry Walden and beguiles his solitude by musing on former residents there, in Revolutionary War times, then early in the nineteenth century, then in his own youth, and so on down to the present—this very winter. "House-Warming" (XIII) similarly moves in time, though more simply. Here Thoreau describes the gradual closing in on him of winter, week by week.

Often a given chapter is built on a series of contrasts. Thus "Sounds" (IV) logically treats natural sounds (1-4), then man-made sounds (5-13), and finally natural sounds again (14-22). The development is that of a sonata, complete even to a kind of coda, since Thoreau ends the chapter by saying "No yard! but unfenced nature reaching up to your very sills. . . . no gate,—no front-yard,—and no path to the civilized world" (22). "Solitude" (V) also has a pattern of contrasts: Thoreau has no sooner described his solitude than he tells us of such natural companions as the seasons, the rain, and pine needles. Next, after he has expressed his delight in his wholesome loneliness, he concludes by saying that he is not alone, since God and nature are his constant companions. Certainly "Higher Laws" (XI) also has a dupal rhythm. Thoreau frankly recognizes the savage side in his nature, but with it is a spiritual side too. He can fish gleefully; yet he admits that fishing hurts his self-respect. "Brute Neighbors" (XII) begins with a dialogue between the Hermit and the Poet, in which partly contrasting and partly complementary attitudes are presented; the chapter continues by describing the savagery of brute nature—recall the battle of the ants—but closes by summarizing the hilarious antics of the loon and finally the love of ducks for Walden waters. Even "The Pond in Winter" (XVI), which surely should present as unified a subject as "Winter Animals" (XV) or "Spring" (XVII), has its contrasts: intellectual doubts vs. natural serenity (XVI, 1-2), the

legend that Walden Pond was bottomless vs. Thoreau's successful sounding of it (6-11), the busy ice-cutters vs. the indo-
lent observer (17-18), and the wintry scene vs. Thoreau's faith
that spring will come (20). Finally, one of the most important
conclusions in "Conclusion" (XVIII) is the paradox that a
change of scene is both good for one and at the same time
ultimately not only unnecessary but impossible (1-3); later in
the same chapter Thoreau contrasts the past with the present,
and the empire with the individual.

Once in a while a given chapter is relatively straightfor-
ward and unitary. For example, "Economy" (I) is topically
autobiographical; it discusses the economic rationale for Thoreau's experiment, together with his thoughts on such necessary
necessities as clothing, shelter, furniture, fire, food, mild work,
and freedom. And so it is with the next two chapters, "Where
I Lived, and What I Lived For" (II) and "Reading" (III),
although the latter contrasts those few who can truly read and
the many who cannot. Likewise, "Winter Animals" (XV)
and "Spring" (XVII) are relatively consistent units.

Finally, what of the pattern of *Walden* as a whole? The
magnificently challenging personality of its author of course
unifies it to a considerable degree. We quickly come to expect
Thoreau to have a personal opinion on almost any and every
subject, and to express it with characteristic vigor and poetry.
In addition, *Walden* has the organic dynamism of a year of
four seasons. Thoreau tells us early in "Where I Lived, and
What I Lived For" that "for convenience" he will "put . . .
the experience of two years into one" (II, 7)—for convenience,
yes, but also for art's sake. The action of the book opens with
Thoreau advancing upon Emerson's arrowy pine trees, axe in
hand, in March. It continues with the building of his house
during the spring. He takes up his residence on the Fourth of
July, and through the summer his miles of beans occupy him.

Only when he feels the chill of fall does he start building his fireplace and chimney. When winter comes, he warms his house, entertains winter visitors, observes the animals, and studies the ice. When winter seriously contracts the land, Thoreau draws in, narrows his field of activity, and ponders. Then spring comes, and it is time for "Conclusion." "Well, there I might live, I said; and there I did live, for an hour, a summer and a winter life; saw how I could let the years run off, buffet the winter through, and see the spring come in" (II, 1). That sentence, like the entire book, has a roll to it like the seasons.

Walden has endless movement within it. The book as a whole may be compared to a wheel of many spokes with Thoreau at the pond the hub. Foreshadowings, repetitions, patterns of key words and images—these all provide lines of force following the spokes of the wheel. Any section of *Walden* will yield the careful reader many examples of its connection to other sections. Take, for an example, the second paragraph of the book (I, 2), which brings up the following crucial topics: Thoreau's critics, poor children, egotism, writers, sincerity, poor students, and Thoreau's message. Thoreau returns to all of these subjects time and time again in the course of later chapters. Or take Paragraph 13, close to the end of "Conclusion" (XVIII): it mentions the rich-poor paradox of the individual life, poverty, the sun, the snow, spring, independence, charity, clothes, friends, the pricelessness of one's thoughts, society, simplicity vs. dissipation, wealth, books, vital experience, and the soul. Certainly that is a list of most of the subjects of *Walden*.

Thoreau often handles the transition from one chapter to the next with great skill. In "Economy" he wrote at length of shelter (I, 42-71). The next chapter, "Where I Lived, and What I Lived For," opens with a consideration of how to choose the site of a house (II, 1-6). "Sounds" follows "Reading," as its opening paragraph reminds us even while Thoreau makes the transition to the next main subject: "But while we are confined to books, though the most select and classic, and read only particular written languages, which are themselves but dialects and provincial, we are in danger of forgetting the language which all things and events speak without metaphor, which alone is copious and standard" (IV, 1)—namely, the sounds of nature. And at the end of the same chapter Thoreau boasts of having "no path to the civilized world" (22); surely this is a good way to direct us to the title of the next chapter, "Solitude" (V). And so on through the whole book. One of the delights of re-reading *Walden* is seeing its innumerable unobtrusive interconnections. Note, for a final instance, what follows the serene observation toward the close of "The Pond in Winter," in which Thoreau has just described the toil of the ice-cutters: "in thirty days more, probably, I shall look from the same window on the pure sea-green Walden water there, . . . and no traces will appear that a man has ever stood there" (XVI, 20). What follows is of course "Spring" (XVII). At the end of "Spring" Thoreau says abruptly that his second year at Walden was similar to his first, and that he left on September 6, 1847. He follows these facts with "Conclusion," in which he tells us that "a change of air and scenery" (XVIII, 1) is necessary to bring out fully the "beautiful and winged life" (18) within each of us. His Walden life, the telling of which is now concluded, resulted in his spiritual rebirth into a "winged" condition. All of these thoughts remind us that in the first paragraph of *Walden* Thoreau stated clearly, "I lived there two years and two months. At present I am a sojourner in civilized life again" (I, 1). So the book has come full circle.

Looking for one more moment at the structure of *Walden* as a whole, we see that just as the words and puns and

images are of two kinds, simple and difficult, and just as the
sentences and paragraphs and individual chapters are of two
kinds, short and long, so the whole book has a pervasive
counterpoint. Part of the time Thoreau is practical and down
to earth, reckoning up his pennies spent and hoeing his inter-
minable beans, nailing into the furring and hoarding his chestnuts, listing the native shrubs and baiting his hook. And part
of the time he is philosophical and abstruse and ethereal,
justifying his experiment, quoting the classics, likening Walden to the sacred Ganges, suppressing the savage in him to
seek the god-like. Three architecturally placed chapters—
"Economy" (I), "Higher Laws" (XI), and "Conclusion"
(XVIII)—support most of his high-soaring spires of thought.
To alter the metaphor, in the course of the book we move
along the entire great chain of being, from stones and sticks
to waves to fish, birds, brute neighbors, and brutish villagers,
to philosopher, poet, and hermit, and at last to demi-gods and
God.

IDEAS IN *WALDEN*

In his "American Scholar" Emerson said that a thinker is subjected to three influences—nature, the past, and the world of action. Thoreau certainly responded to the influence of nature, studied the past and applied what he learned from books to the present, and had innumerable things to say about society. In fact, most of his ideas can be subsumed under the three main topics of nature, knowledge, and society. Thoreau found that by keeping himself natural and simple in society and out, and by filling his leisure with solitary saunters through nature, observation of natural processes, and reading of eclectically chosen masters, he could develop a positive message which it behooved society to listen to.

Nature kept Thoreau simple and natural. He urges us to "spend one day as deliberately as Nature, and not be thrown off the track by every nutshell and mosquito's wing that falls on the rails" (II, 22). More specifically, he explains, "Every morning was a cheerful invitation to make my life of equal simplicity, and I may say innocence, with Nature herself. I have been as sincere a worshipper of Aurora as the Greeks. I got up early and bathed in the pond; that was a religious exercise, and one of the best things which I did" (14). So that we will be sure to understand, he says more stridently, "I say, let your affairs be as two or three, and not a hundred or a thousand; instead of a million count half a dozen, and keep your account on your thumb-nail" (17).

If we do so, we can learn to respond more naturally to sensory impressions, to say with Thoreau one day, "This is a delicious evening, when the whole body is one sense, and imbibes delight through every pore. I go and come with a strange liberty in Nature, a part of herself" (V, 1). To those who might argue that Thoreau, being exceptionally ascetic and refined, was more capable of such a response to nature than most busy people today, he has a ready if exaggerative answer: "I never dreamed of any enormity greater than I have committed. I never knew, and never shall know, a worse man than myself" (I, 108). He had a savage nature too, he confesses, but learned to channel it toward God.

God's handiwork was all about Thoreau, and he took great delight in studying it. Emerson's description of him in the process one day is charming. "He wore a straw hat, stout shoes, strong gray trousers, to brave scrub-oaks and smilax, and to climb a tree for a hawk's or a squirrel's nest. He waded into the pool for the water-plants, and his strong legs were no insignificant part of his armor. On the day I speak of he . . . drew out of his breast-pocket his diary, and read the names of all the plants that should bloom on this day, whereof he kept account as a banker when his notes fall due. . . . He thought that, if waked up from a trance, in this swamp, he could tell by the plants what time of the year it was within two days." As readers of *Walden* know, Thoreau noted with exactness the depth and temperature of the pond and the dates when it was first open during different springs. He recorded with a painter's vision details concerning trees, fish, birds, and animals. He has been praised rightly for his accurate if haphazard contributions of meteorology, limnology, phenology, and ecology, all of which in his time were undeveloped branches of science.

This love of nature led Thoreau to respect the Indians. As a youth he glided through the forests and stalked game like an aborigine. Later he taught his pupils Indian lore. He always admired the woodcraft and manners of Indians, who he said were unconstrained in nature, were her inhabitants rather than her guests. He could find Indian arrowheads more successfully than other searchers for them. He liked the savor of Indian names for places and streams near Concord. He took notes on Indians in New England and in Minnesota for a book which he did not have the time even to start. However, shortly before his death, Thoreau gradually came to deplore the spiritual and aesthetic atrophy of the typical Indian, and it might be justly said that he was mainly concerned with the Indian as a woodsman and as a living contrast to the urban white man.

Thoreau enjoyed talking with hunters and trappers. In *Walden* we read, "There is a period in the history of the individual, as of the race, when the hunters are the 'best men,' as the Algonquins called them. I cannot but pity the boy who has never fired a gun; he is no more humane, while his education has been sadly neglected. This was my answer with respect to those youths who were bent on this pursuit, trusting that they would soon outgrow it" (XI, 3). Hunting was thus a necessary step in the education of the natural boy and man. Thoreau's most complete character sketch in *Walden* is that of the French-Canadian woodchopper; yet, as with the spiritually and artistically immature Indian, so with the delightful chopper. He was spirited, considerate, trusting; but, though he could give the rudiments of good answers to questions, he was really more animal than human. He was, in short, merely a primitive.

Thoreau did not espouse primitivism. If he had, he would have stayed in the woods and not emerged to visit the Harvard library or to spend a night in jail. Nor, probably, would he have read Homer at Walden, kept such a civilized journal there, and planned a long account of his experiment. Primitivism was agreeable to him only to this extent—he was willing to spend a couple of years mainly in nature to see how very easy it was to live simply, to front only the essentials, and to reduce his denominator, in order to return to society armed with suggestions. After all, *Walden* begins with "Economy" and ends with "Conclusion." In addition, the typical primitive does not hold with progress. Thoreau may joke that he owned only a tent before he built his hut at the pond, and so "With this more substantial shelter about me, I had made some progress toward settling in the world" (II, 9). But his whole aim in going to Walden was to make some progress there, and then turn around and go back to Concord better than he was when he had started. He borrowed an axe to build his house, "but I returned it [he explains] sharper than I received it" (I, 60). He returned sharper too. Never the smug primitive, he saw each day as a new chance to "strik[e] at the root" rather than "at the branches of evil" (I, 106). If he sometimes seems like a primitive, perhaps it is because we cannot understand his unique form of striking at the root of evil.

Little more need be said here of Thoreau's love of nature. Thoreau never felt alone in natural solitude. He was always in the presence of that "old settler and original proprietor, who is reported to have dug Walden Pond, and stoned it, and fringed it with pine woods" (VI, 16). And Mother Nature was his most welcome guest there. Emily Dickinson could sing, "Inebriate of air am I, / And debauchee of dew"; as Thoreau similarly puts it, "Morning air! If men will not drink of this at the fountain-head of the sky, why, then, we must bottle up some and sell it in shops, for the benefit of those who have lost their subscription ticket to morning time in this world" (V, 18). Those who seek health, need nature; those who learn to love nature, gain health. Thoreau relished tramping through the woods more than any other physical activity, recorded that he could not preserve his health and equanimity without a daily four-hour saunter in the country, and even thought that choosing a particular goal for a walk on a given day in a given season could be made into a science. The beauty of it all is that Thoreau did not selfishly take these walks, but instead shared them with his journal, and hence with us.

Like Emerson, Thoreau used his forays into nature in order to refine his philosophical concepts. As he grew older he may have deplored his tendency to record mere data at the expense of a dwindling desire to transcend the merely sensory; yet until the end he was a thorough Transcendentalist. Surely the main point of "Higher Laws" (XI) is that all persons should "work . . . out the beast, / And let the tiger die" in themselves, as Tennyson puts it.

Transcendentalism stemmed from neo-Platonic philosophy, the writings of German idealist philosophers, and Oriental mysticism. Thoreau agreed with the Platonists who held that spirit transcends matter and that out of physical laws governing inanimate and organic nature one can generate laws concerning spiritual values. He agreed with the idealists that faith and intuition can teach us more than mere cold intellect. He used various Hindu writings to try to reconcile spirit and matter, to try to make monistic the flawed dualism which plagued all the Transcendentalists, including Emerson.

Although Plato is mentioned on only two occasions in Walden (III, 10; VI, 13), his idealism informs much of the book, for example, when Thoreau moves from his discussion of reading to a statement that "we are in danger of forgetting the language which all things and events speak without metaphor, which alone is copious and standard" (IV, 1). By this suggestion Thoreau is stating his desire to get at reality first-hand, not indirectly through mere books. The nature-writer John Burroughs once explained this Platonism by saying that Thoreau was less interested in a given pursued bird than in "a bird behind the bird,—for a mythology to shine through his ornithology." Perhaps Platonism can best account for the following teasing lines from Thoreau: "I long ago lost a hound, a bay horse, and a turtle-dove, and am still on their trail. Many are the travellers I have spoken concerning them, describing their tracks and what calls they answered to. I have met one or two who had heard the hound, and the tramp of the horse, and even seen the dove disappear behind a cloud, and they seemed as anxious to recover them as if they had lost them themselves" (I, 24). Thoreau felt incomplete and sought his other self, his better half, all through his life. In addition, he surely was the gadfly of Concord, as Plato's Socrates was of Athens.

German idealism evidently came to Thoreau quite circuitously, through Carlyle and Emerson, especially the latter, whose *Nature*, 1836, enraptured him when it spoke of discovering one's essential inner nature through delight in beauteous and moral outer nature. Thoreau owned an English translation of Johann Ritter von Zimmermann's *On Solitude*, which may have influenced "Solitude" (V) in *Walden*. But to the *Sturm und Drang* movement generally, Thoreau was unresponsive: it encouraged an abandonment of the intellect to the emotions, a surrender of the head to the heart, which Thoreau thought was the death of the spirit. Note that after he commented on the immortality of sweet Walden water when frozen, contrasted to the quick putridity of warm water, he added as though to criticize nine-tenths of his romantic contemporaries, including Nathaniel Hawthorne and Herman Melville even, the following sardonic lines: "It is commonly said that this is the difference between the affections and the intellect" (XVI, 19). While Hawthorne in *The Scarlet Letter,* 1850, was condemning Roger Chillingworth for cold-headedly violating the sanctity of Arthur Dimmesdale's heart, and while Melville was voicing his preference for the heart over the head —"To the dogs with the head! I stand for the heart"—Thoreau chastely restrained his emotional make-up and consciously sublimated. "By turns [he wrote] our purity inspires and our impurity casts us down. He is blessed who is assured that the animal is dying out in him day by day, and the divine being established" (XI, 11).

As for Oriental mysticism, Thoreau's interest in it is easily documented by recourse to his journal but is perhaps sufficiently attested by simply noting that in *Walden* he writes, "How much more admirable the Bhagvat-Geeta than all the ruins of the East! Towers and temples are the luxury of princes. A simple and independent mind does not toil at the bidding of any prince" (I, 79). This shows that Thoreau places thought above thing. Further, he tells us that when spring begins to melt the Walden ice, "I bathe my intellect in the stupendous and cosmogonal philosophy of the Bhagvat-Geeta, since whose composition years of the gods have elapsed, and in comparison with which our modern world and its literature seem puny and trivial" (XVI, 21). And throughout the book Thoreau shares with us his Oriental ecstasy, insight, and oblivion. He tells us half-humorously that the Poet interrupted his reclusive mystical state: "What was it that I was thinking of? It was a very hazy day. I will just try these three sentences of Confut-see [Confucius]; they may fetch that state about again. I know not whether it was the dumps or a budding ecstasy" (XII, 5). The entire document is full of Oriental insight, perhaps the most important being the notion that through advancing in the direction of one's dreams one can experience a spiritual rebirth. Advancing toward one's castle in the air or wedging through the slush and mud of so-called life to the solid bottom necessarily obliges one to become oblivious of sick surface realities. "Why should we live with such hurry and waste of life? We are determined to be starved before we are hungry. . . . As for *work,* we haven't any of consequence. We have the St. Vitus' dance . . ." (II, 18). Further, advancing toward his mystical thoughts obliged Thoreau on occasion to become oblivious even of beauteous nature about him.

> Sometimes, in a summer morning, having taken my accustomed bath, I sat in my sunny doorway from sunrise till noon, rapt in a revery, amidst the pines and hickories and sumachs, in undisturbed solitude and stillness, while the birds sang around or flitted noiseless through the house, until by the sun falling in at my west window, or the noise of some travellers' wagon on the distant highway, I was reminded of the lapse of time. I grew in those seasons like corn in the night, and they were far better than any work of the hands would have been. (IV, 2)

However, Oriental though Thoreau was in these ways, he obviously did not hold with Hindu asceticism. What he loved essentially was life; what he sought was the simplest, sanest formula for living it. "I did not wish to live what was not life, living is so dear; nor did I wish to practise resignation, unless it was quite necessary. I wanted to live deep and suck out all the marrow of life . . ." (II, 16).

    In two main respects, then, Thoreau was a Transcendentalist. He was a solitary worshipper of nature, and he trusted that his self-reliant responses to all things would lead him to beauty, goodness, and truth. But he was not a thorough-going

Transcendentalist. The shallow optimism which disfigures
Transcendentalism in the modern view, he never accepted. He
knew well that "The mass of men lead lives of quiet desperation" (I, 9) with no Emersonian compensations at all. Sneer-
ing untranscendentally, he found much wrong in "this slimy,
beastly life" (XI, 9). He concluded that "Only that day dawns
to which we are awake" and that "not every John and Jonathan will realize all this" (XVIII, 19). Those who are dead
to nature's beauties, those who claw cranberries off their
bushes for monetary profit only, those who call their muck-
heaps model farms and make burdened beasts of themselves—
these are Johns and Jonathans for whom no transcendental
day will ever dawn. Thoreau also admitted the presence of
evil in the world. He did not believe, as his friend Emerson
did, that every aspect of evil was compensated for by an
opposite good and that good luck had to be paid for by in-
creased responsibilities. Thoreau believed both that evil was
rampant in society and that one could enjoy ebriosity in nature
with never a compensatory hangover. In addition, he differed
from the Transcendentalists in having grave doubts concerning such material evidences of progress as the postal service,
urban development, unrestricted immigration, western expansion, the practical fruits of science, and that snorting monster
the omnivorous railroad. He did not optimistically or even
just tolerantly feel that these changes contained the seeds of
betterment.

In several respects Thoreau was not Transcendental or
anti-Transcendental but instead was simply in the main stream
of western romanticism. Thus, he was eclectic and contradic-
tory. He revered the classics and the scriptures of faraway
India and yet celebrated the low, the common, the here and
now. He ridiculed academicians and profess-ers; yet he availed
himself coolly enough of the professionally managed Harvard

College library. He loathed institutions and yet supported Lyceum educational programs and some professional abolitionists. He prided himself on his classically faultless logic, planned aspects of his life rationally enough, and argued orally and in writing with all the rhetorical tricks of the trade; yet he avoided any systematic and definitive statement of his position, preferring ambivalent poetics instead.

All of this is undoubtedly owing to the fact that—like Coleridge, Keats, Emerson, and Hawthorne, among many others— he saw his personal philosophy the same way he did houses, flora and fauna, poems, Waldens, and life itself, that is, organically. He compares houses to "the tenement of the shellfish" (I, 58), adding a little later, "What of architectural beauty I now see, I know has gradually grown from within outward, out of the necessities and character of the indweller, who is the only builder,—out of some unconscious truthfulness, and nobleness" (68). All living, evolving forms are poems, and the only time Thoreau uses the word *poem* in *Walden* is when he writes ecstatically that "The morning wind forever blows, the poem of creation is uninterrupted" (II, 8). He sees the pond as a living, changing creature which through days and seasons and longer cycles of nature gently suspires and inspires. The rippling dimples on its surface thus become "the gentle pulsing of its life, the heaving of its breast" (IX, 18). Thoreau is ten times as concerned with the example of the noble poet's life than with his poetry. In fact, he once wrote,

> My life has been the poem I would have writ,
> But I could not both live and utter it.

Nonetheless he saw himself as a writer with a mission. Therefore, he used his solitary time in nature to find beauty, truth, and a way of life which he could then discuss with

mankind. In order to make his message palatable, he spiced
Walden with some of the finest humor by any American
before Mark Twain. He vivified it with glowing pictorial
effects, deepened it with subtle musical rhythms, and built
it as sturdily and functionally as his little house. Perhaps he
only certified its permanence by his tantalizing paradoxes
and conundrums, which were consciously woven in, since he
tells us early in the recital, "You will pardon some obscurities,
for there are more secrets in my trade than in most men's,
and yet not voluntarily kept, but inseparable from its very
nature" (I, 23). Among other things, *Walden* is a parable
for the would-be writer. It discusses the nature of his sacri-
fices, ways he should handle his raw material, varieties of
literary tempers, and the unity of all creation.

Next, the burden of Thoreau's message to the world.
Walden contains a surprising amount of practical advice. To
begin, Thoreau encourages parents to let their children hunt
and fish, so that they can learn about nature in the most
effortless and pleasant way possible. He urges clean housekeeping through descriptions of his own simple methods and,
negatively, through the humorous picture of the slovenly
Mrs. Field, "with the never absent mop in one hand, and yet
no effects of it visible anywhere" (X, 3). He indirectly suggested that Field himself mend his ways and work less so
that he would need less food; in addition, Thoreau might not
have minded if Field could have known his thoughts on
chastity and hence brought into his boggy environment fewer
cone-headed infants than the swarm which he obviously
could not provide for.

Thoreau regularly advised practical education. He
preached learning by doing, whether it was learning about
knives, navigation, or life, rather than expensively studying
mere theory under a so-called professor. When he was a

teacher himself, he practiced a gentle pragmatic system which was notably successful and far ahead of his times; when he came to write *Walden,* he must have remembered that success. Also he advocated adult-education programs, because he felt that one was never too old to learn.

Ever a friend to fellow-students, he was also a friend to all who would join him in loving life. He movingly describes his friendship with the woodchopper, his sympathy for the mentally retarded fellow who came out to visit him, and his wondrous joy in the philosopher, the "blue-robed man . . . [whom] Nature cannot spare" (XIV, 21). Far from advocating complete solitude, Thoreau like Melville's Redburn was always on the lookout for an "immaculate friend."

To get the most from life, Thoreau advocated reducing our needs and consequently the time necessarily spent providing for them. In his passion for simplicity, he even campaigned for reversing the Biblical formula, that is, to have a six-day Sabbath and toilfully sweat only on the seventh day each week. Yet it should be added at once that, far from disliking work, Thoreau relished it when it was meaningful. He took his own sweet time when he built his house by the pond, because he wanted to savor each stage of the process: "I made no haste in my work, but rather made the most of it" (I, 63). He took pride in any honorable work he agreed to perform, and advises us to do the same, "so . . . that you can wake up in the night and think of your work with satisfaction" (XVIII, 14). He also rejoiced in his ability to perform commendably at a great variety of occupations and as a result feared the inevitable advent of labor specialization. It should be added that Thoreau did not do his minimum of toil so that he could loll in the mild sunshine for hours and days on end, nor does he advise us to reduce our needs to this ignoble and slothful end. "Who knows what beautiful

and winged life . . . may unexpectedly come forth?" (18).
Only productive leisure can warm such a life into being. A
less slothful retirement than Thoreau's to Walden can hardly
be imagined. His example there should be object-lesson
enough for those who deplore the coming of automation as
the dread creator of too much free time.

As we have been partly seeing, Thoreau inveighed
against most institutions, including school and college boards,
organized churches, official movements such as the abolitionist cause, commercial enterprise, and institutionalized govern-
ments at all levels. The man who felt that metallurgy should
be learned by mining and smelting, navigation by sailing,
and natural science by hiking would necessarily have little
respect for curricula, credits, and sheepskins. The pantheist
who called the beech groves his temples and preferred the
sound of church bells when sifted through miles of pine
needles could not be expected to surrender his spiritual independence to any sect or sectarian. Though Thoreau tells us
of "One real runaway slave . . . whom [he] helped to forward toward the north star" (VI, 16), in his Walden phase
he saw almost all men as slaves and therefore wrote little of
the abolitionist movement then. Later, when he made up
his mind, quite independently, to throw his weight alongside
of the abolitionists, he did so in ways which often made them
wonder which side he was really on. He once upset the
organized abolitionists by announcing that he was going to
lecture on John Brown. Emerson reports on his plan as follows: "The Republican Committee, the Abolitionist Committee, sent him word that it was premature and not advisable.
He replied,—'I did not send to you for advice, but to
announce that I am to speak.' The hall was filled at an early
hour . . ." Commercial enterprises, whether transportation or
ruthlessly efficient agricultural or ice-vending businesses, Tho-

reau also distrusted. The moment a person stopped letting nature feed him like a generous mother and instead organized bands of hirelings to ravish her, the whole fabric of life was wrenched. For "trade curses everything it handles; and though you trade in messages from Heaven, the whole curse of trade attaches to the business" (I, 97). Obviously the man who went to jail rather than pay any tax to his government, disapproved of the way that government was drifting. However, Thoreau did not favor anarchy; all he wanted was for the government to remain a means of helping its people attain desirable ends. A good government could support adult-education programs ahead of one more unnecessary bridge and thus help make the common school uncommonly good (III, 12). It could at the same time institute conservation programs, sane road-building programs, and so on and on. But when the government became a leviathan which crushed the individual, it was time, Thoreau averred, to declare his personal independence of it.

In short, when it came to a choice between advancing in the direction of his dreams or knuckling down to institutions, Thoreau like Socrates listened only to his inner voice. It was for this reason that he distrusted reform movements organized by committed groups and imposed from outside upon others. He agreed with Hawthorne that the first thing to be reformed was the individual human heart. Thoreau reformed his heart at Walden, in fact was utterly reborn there. He strove for our rebirth too.

It cannot be sufficiently emphasized, however, that Thoreau did not want anyone to read him and then drop out of school or tear up his diploma, borrow an axe and get arrested for squatting somewhere, work six weeks a year and vegetate the other forty-six, loftily go to jail for declining to register for the draft or pay his income tax, or in any other way be literally and narrowly Thoreauvian in a different century. To do so would be to dishonor *Walden*. Toward the end of the book Thoreau tells us of the path he quickly wore from his door to the pond; years later he noted that it was still quite distinct. He goes on, suggestively, "It is true, I fear, that others may have fallen into it, and so helped to keep it open. The surface of the earth is soft and impressible by the feet of men; and so with the paths which the mind travels. How worn and dusty, then, must be the highways of the world, how deep the ruts of tradition and conformity!" (XVIII, 4). Is he not telling us that paradoxically we would be following him best by not following him? Is he not saying that we can be most like him by listening not to his voice but our own? To honor Thoreau best, one should have a worthy aim, simplify his life, and work honorably to make his dream come true.

SOME OF THOREAU'S
OTHER WORKS

In addition to *Walden,* which with his journal represents Thoreau's most vital literary effort, readers are referred to the following works, which taken together convincingly show his steady development and undisputed importance.

A Winter Walk was published in the *Dial* in 1843. It is a gentle familiar essay, following an outline imposed by a walk in the Walden Pond area from just before dawn until evening during a pleasantly wintry day. Many of the lyrical descriptions anticipate sections in *Walden.* The tone is not broken by any social commentary. The essay simply shows a youthful Thoreau responding to nature with sympathy and delight.

Thomas Carlyle and His Works, 1847. This essay is the only long piece of literary criticism that Thoreau ever tried. It discusses Carlyle's life briefly and then analyzes his style, tone, and philosophy. Thoreau's essay is valuable less for its comments on the content of Carlyle's many works than for its occasional insight into elements of his style, notably humor, which Thoreau suggestively calls "a main attraction in these books."

A Week on the Concord and Merrimack Rivers, 1849. Thoreau and his beloved brother John took a trip by rowboat to the White Mountains of New Hampshire and back. They were gone from Saturday, August 31, to Friday, September 13, 1839. Thoreau started writing a book about the excursion not long thereafter. He progressed only sporadically for a while. Then John died in 1842 of lockjaw, after which Thoreau decided to make his book a fraternal tribute. At the outset of it he writes, "Be thou my Muse, my Brother." He went to Walden Pond in part to guarantee himself uninterrupted time to complete *A Week*. Although it evidently was nearly finished in 1846, delays and disappointments held up its publication until 1849. Then it was issued at Thoreau's expense and sold very badly for years thereafter. *A Week* begins with a brief introductory description of Concord River. The main book follows with a chapter devoted to each day of the week-long trip beginning with Saturday and continuing through the following Friday. Curiously, just as Thoreau later compressed two years into the one-year structure of *Walden,* so in *A Week* he compressed two weeks into one. Significantly, Sunday is the nominal subject of the second chapter and not in any sense the culmination of Thoreau's week; in fact, Thoreau seems anxious to record his preference for Far Eastern scriptures over the Old and New Testaments. (He calls the Bible "an old book" and the story of Adam and Eve a "fable" in *Walden* [I, 5, 42], seemingly in a conscious effort to alienate his conservative readers.) The week proceeds pleasantly, as the brothers sail and row down the Concord to the Merrimack, up into New Hampshire, and back home again. But the account is marred in the view of many by its numerous capricious digressions, interpolated essays, poems, philosophical and literary discussions, and the like. The result is a bookish and youthful effort, notable for a sense of immediacy, a tone of optimism, and a heavy load of imperfectly controlled erudition. The travel sections have been separated and successfully published alone. The verse is now part of Thoreau's *Collected Poems*. It is especially illuminating to see by reading *A Week* that Thoreau as early as 1839 was studying and thinking and living along lines which were to converge at Walden Pond a few years later.

Civil Disobedience was first published in 1849 in *Aesthetic Papers,* edited by Nathaniel Hawthorne's sister-in-law Elizabeth Peabody, a Salem Transcendentalist and bookseller. There it was called "Resistance to Civil Government." In republications after Thoreau's death it was retitled "Civil Disobedience." The essay is Thoreau's most famous. Its influence has gone around the world. Ironically, Thoreau the arch-individualist was the intellectual progenitor of Mahatma Gandhi's gigantic passive-resistance movement, participated in by countless thousands of united individuals in India. And there is something poetically gratifying in the fact that one century after the Civil War, the social, economic, and political causes of which Thoreau so eloquently deplored, his philosophy of civil disobedience became an instrument in the civil rights agitation of 1963 and 1964. Thoreau begins his essay not merely by agreeing that that government is best which governs least but also by extending the motto as follows: "That government is best which governs not at all." What Thoreau wants until men are prepared for absence of government is a better government, and at once. When a government is tyrannical or unendurably inefficient, its people have the right to rebel. And now is the time in the United States, Thoreau adds, since a sixth of the population is enslaved and American soldiers have unjustly overrun Mexico. Instead of saying that they dislike what is going on but dare not disobey the admittedly unjust laws of the land, Thoreau says that honest men should obey their own consciences, withdraw their support from the government, and go to jail if need be. "Under a government which imprisons any unjustly, the true place for a just man is also a prison." If a large enough group of people,

even though it is still comparatively a minority, passively re-
sists in this fashion, "it is irresistible when it clogs by its whole
weight. If the alternative is to keep all just men in prison, or
give up war and slavery, the State will not hesitate which to
choose." Next Thoreau describes his own experience of being
jailed for refusing to pay his poll-tax. "I felt as if I alone of
all my townsmen had paid my tax." Therefore, though behind
bars, stone, and mortar, he felt uniquely free that night, for
his intellect and whole moral being remained free. In the
morning he was released because "some one interfered and
paid that tax," which misguided act Thoreau deplored as an
instance of abetting injustice. Thoreau wants it clearly understood that he does not enjoy being a non-comformist. He
would welcome a chance to obey the law. And perhaps when
more progress has been made, he can do so. But progress will
prove difficult, because our statesmen and legislators only
expediently modify our political institutions and defend our
Constitution, whereas they should take a higher view, utterly
reform many positions, and aggressively (not defensively) lead
the people. Thoreau is unwilling to abide by the Constitution
or even the Bible but instead wants to make his pilgrimage to
the fountainhead of their inspiration. In conclusion, Thoreau
notes that man's progress from absolute monarchy to limited
monarchy and then to democracy is based upon respect for
the individual, who is "the basis of the empire." But perhaps
democracy is not the final step in all this evolution. "Is it not
possible to take a step further towards recognizing and organ-
izing the rights of man?" No government will be really free
and enlightened until it recognizes "the individual as a higher
and independent power, from which all its own power and
authority are derived . . ." Then we would have true justice,
individualism, and neighborliness. "A State which bore this
kind of fruit, and suffered it to drop off as fast as it ripened,

would prepare the way for a still more perfect and glorious State, which also I have imagined, but not yet anywhere seen."

Slavery in Massachusetts appeared in 1854. Thoreau delivered this vitriolic protest against injustice at a Fourth of July anti-slavery convention in Framingham, Massachusetts. The particular causes of his discontent were three: in 1851 Thomas Sims, a runaway slave, was seized in Boston, tried, and returned to his master in Georgia; in May, 1854, the Kansas-Nebraska Bill was passed, thus in effect repealing the Missouri Compromise and guaranteeing that Congress would not intervene in the western territories; and in June, 1854, Anthony Burns, another runaway slave, was ordered returned from Boston to his master in Virginia. Thoreau begins his address by lashing out at his hypocritical fellow citizens of Massachusetts for worrying about slavery far away when it is right in their own state. "I had thought that the house was on fire, and not the prairie . . ." He then disavows any loyalty to the state governor: "He was no Governor of mine. He did not govern me." Next he vilifies the Fugitive Slave Law, urging that it be trampled under foot, "and Webster, its maker, with it, like the dirt-bug and its ball." Then he pours his most corrosive sarcasm on the press. "Could slavery suggest a more complete servility than some of these journals exhibit? Is there any dust which their conduct does not lick, and make fouler still with its slime? . . . When I have taken up this paper with my cuffs turned up, I have heard the gurgling of the sewer through every column. I have felt that I was handling a paper picked out of the public gutters, a leaf from the gospel of the gambling-house, the groggery and the brothel, harmonizing with the gospel of the Merchants' Exchange." Finally, he concludes by repeating thoughts which he had eloquently expressed in "Civil Disobedience" earlier. Each inhabitant of

Massachusetts should dissolve his union with it if it continues any longer to tolerate slaveholding and servility within its borders. Thoreau feels such a sense of outrage that he closes by reporting that his joy in nature herself is temporarily sullied—"We walk to lakes to see our serenity reflected in them; when we are not serene, we go not to them"—until he takes a lesson from a flower springing out of the slimy muck. "I secured a water-lily . . . It is the emblem of purity. . . . It reminds me that Nature has been partner to no Missouri Compromise. I scent no compromise in the fragrance of the water-lily. . . . In it, the sweet, the pure, the innocent, are wholly sundered from the obscene and baleful. I do not scent in this the time-serving irresolution of a Massachusetts Governor, nor of a Boston mayor. So behave that the odor of your actions may enhance the general sweetness of the atmosphere, that when we behold or scent a flower, we may not be reminded how inconsistent your deeds are with it; for all odor is but one form of advertisement of a moral quality, and if fair actions had not been performed, the lily would not swell sweet. The foul slime stands for the sloth and vice of man, the decay of humanity; the fragrant flower that springs from it, for the purity and courage which are immortal."

A Plea for Captain John Brown was published in 1860. On October 16, 1859, Captain John Brown attacked Harper's Ferry. Two days later he was captured. His swift trial ended October 31. But even before it did, Thoreau on October 30 called a meeting at the Concord Town Hall, ringing the bell himself, at which he read his impassioned and persuasive plea for the fiery but utterly sincere fanatic. He repeated it twice within a few days. John Brown was nonetheless executed, on December 2. Thoreau's lecture was published in 1860. It is uncannily moving. In it Thoreau denounces the business-as-usual government, and criticizes church and press and all timid individuals everywhere for not speaking out in favor of John Brown. He repeatedly compares Brown to Christ, cleanser of the materialistic temple, would-be savior of four million enslaved Negroes, outfacer of modern Pilates, and a victim soon to be crucified. The speech is in no sense a plea for Brown's life but simply for his character. The lecture begins by describing Brown's past, his nature, and his deeds. Thoreau sees the attack on Harper's Ferry as an event of almost unparalleled significance. A high-principled, peerless man was willing to die striking a blow there against those who tyrannize over the oppressed and defenseless. We cannot leave their defense to the existing government. The only government Thoreau recognizes is "that power that establishes justice in the land," whereas what we have is "a monster of a government . . . where the noblest faculties of the mind, and the *whole* heart, are not *represented*. A semi-tiger or ox, stalking over the earth, with its heart taken out and the top of its brain shot away." Thoreau then praises Brown as a unique hero who teaches us how to die, and live. Then he concludes by predicting that poets will sing of John Brown, that painters will paint his trial, and that one day "at least the present form of Slavery shall be no more here." The speech seethes with Thoreau's at times uncontrolled and almost hysterical indignation. It is a volcanic denunciation of the pusillanimity of a clear national majority —of moral cowards. Thoreau also wrote "After the Death of John Brown" as a speech on the day Brown was hanged, and "The Last Days of John Brown" as a speech on the occasion of Brown's burial the following July.

The Succession of Forest Trees, 1860. Thoreau read this essay as a paper before the Middlesex Agricultural Society and then published it later the same fall. The short work scientifically discusses the propagation of forest trees, how "when a pine wood was cut down an oak one commonly sprang up, and *vice versa*," and the need of forest management. Through it all, however, Thoreau lets his irrepressible humor filter pleasantly, beginning in the first sentence: "Every man is entitled to come to Cattle-Show, even a transcendentalist . . ."

Walking, 1862. Thoreau put this charming essay into final form out of journal entries and lectures. It was published a month after he died, which fact makes something very moving out of its last three paragraphs. They tell of the paradisal joy he and a companion once felt when they saw a kind of morning sunlight break out of cold and gray skies one November afternoon, upon which "every wood and rising ground gleamed like the boundary of Elysium." He closes by hoping that such a golden light will shine into all minds and hearts one day. The whole essay is a delightful ramble over a variety of subjects, such as the pleasures of walking, the inexhaustible possibilities for exploration in the countryside around Concord, the fact that while light comes from the orient East fruit comes from our tropically rich and teeming West, and the joy Thoreau feels in the musky wildness of America. The essay has no more apparent plan than a spontaneous hike through the woods. Perhaps for that reason it reveals much of the essential Thoreau, whose tone here is unusually gay and mellow.

Wild Apples, 1862. This thrilling essay was first presented as a lecture in 1860, with ringing success. Thoreau revised and expanded it later, adding material, for example, about crab-apples he saw in Minnesota in 1861. The work was published posthumously. "Wild Apples" is a captivating combination of accurate scientific observation, impressive erudition and humorous pseudo-erudition, homely bits of autobiographical narrative, and dazzling baroque style. It should also be mentioned that on one level it is a little parable in justification of Thoreau's wild ways. Like the wild apple, Thoreau saw himself as transcendentally sturdy, undomesticatable, naturally tending away from the urban, and perhaps too acrid for most people's taste. But, he seems to add gaily, how can one be critical when his wild walks and patient journal entries bear such fruit as this hypnotic essay?

Life Without Principle, 1863. In his journal Thoreau often talked to himself on the subject of earning a living without compromising one's principles. He put together his thoughts into a lecture called "Getting a Living," with this for its text: "For what shall it profit a man, if he shall gain the whole world, and lose his own soul?" (Mark 8:36; see also Matthew 16:26). Thoreau revised his lecture for publication shortly before he died. It was printed a year later as "Life With Principle," a title assigned to it by the editor. The essay is hard-hitting, forthright, and disquieting. It attacks the perpetual busy-ness of Americans. "I think that there is nothing, not even crime, more opposed to poetry, to philosophy, ay, to life itself, than this incessant business." If Thoreau conforms and works in a conventional way, he will be commended; but if he devotes his energies to pursuits of ultimately greater profit to himself, he will be called an idler. Thoreau insists that one should not work merely for money, not merely to hold a job, "but to perform well a certain work . . ." Yet few are employed so. Too often people envy those who inherit wealth, those who are clever at amassing money, and those who chance to strike it rich in the raffles of the world. Gold diggers rush to California and Australia, but they should sink a shaft into their own thoughts, and find gold there. Many people compromise their morals in getting their bread. They grow coarse and refuse to discuss essentials, preferring instead the trivia of the daily news. Instead of listening, however, to "the profane and stale revelation of the barroom and the police court," we should prefer "the mountain brooks, the Parnassian streams." "Read not the Times. Read the Eternities." We call ourselves free of King George but remain "the slaves of King Prejudice." Our souls are eaten up by "our gross bodies." We call ourselves cultured and mature in America now, but "we are essentially provincial still, . . . because we are warped and narrowed by an exclusive devotion to trade and commerce and manufactures and agriculture and the like, which are but means, and not the end." In a country placing great value on slavery and material exports, how can a legislator take pride in his calling or a citizen be truly patriotic? We will produce "heroes, saints, poets, philosophers, and redeemers" only when we want "illumination more than sugar-plums." It is suggestive to compare this posthumously published work by Thoreau with his *Walden*. The two contain the same basic ideas, the same rugged individualism, and similar techniques—intentionally meandering outline, erudition, word play, imagery— but the short lecture is more distilled, is almost a "Now Hear This" from beyond the grave. Its plea for self-trust and for a dismissal of materialism is challenging today.

The Maine Woods, 1864. This posthumously published book is composed of three long essays: "Ktaadn," which appeared in magazine form in 1848; "Chesuncook," which appeared in magazine form in 1858; and "The Allegash and East Branch," which Thoreau tried to put into final form from his journal entries shortly before he died. "Ktaadn" is based on his trip to Mount Katahdin, Maine, in 1846 during his second summer at Walden. "Chesuncook" recounts his trip to Maine in 1853. "The Allegash and East Branch" deals with his last Maine trip, in 1857. In addition there is an appendix concerning Maine trees, flowers and shrubs, plants, birds, and quadrupeds, proper hiking clothes and equipment, and finally a careful list of Indian words noted. Thoreau's friend Channing edited the three essays and the rest and saw to their publication two years after Thoreau died. Since he died before he saw the book in any kind of definitive form, the result is pardonably disunified, repetitious, and at times seemingly careless. *The Maine Woods,* nonetheless, is a valuable travel book. Thoreau went to Maine principally to learn Indian lore. In this he was aided by two different Indian guides there. The book is enriched by much information from them. Undoubtedly Thoreau would have compiled a separate, full-length book on Indians if he had lived longer. The individual sections of the completed work are chronologically ordered for the most part, imposing a degree of narrative coherence. The tone is mainly sober and serious, as suits the informational and descriptive intention, but occasionally Thoreau's humor breaks through like sunlight in woody depths.

Cape Cod, 1865. Thoreau took four trips to Cape Cod— in 1849 with Channing, in 1850 alone, in 1855 with Channing again, and in 1857 alone again. In 1850 and 1851 he lectured most successfully on Cape Cod, which he called "the bared and bended arm of Massachusetts." The first four chapters of what became the book *Cape Cod* were published in magazine form in 1855; two other chapters, in 1864. The entire work, ten chapters in all, was edited from Thoreau's incompletely revised manuscripts by his sister Sophia and his friend Channing, and was published three years after his death. This book has more unity and charm than *The Maine Woods.* Its outline follows Thoreau's first trip; but at the same time, the work includes material gleaned from the second and third trips, though not from the fourth. The book is freighted with a typical amount of historical and literary erudition. Much better are Thoreau's own keen-sighted observations of the tough

terrain and its rugged occupants. Best of all here is Thoreau's
personality, which—as is usual, to be sure, in all of his travel
books—shines through with the purity of his honor and the
sparkle of his wit.

A Yankee in Canada, 1853, 1866. Thoreau took a one-week
trip into Canada with Channing in 1850. Three years later he
published in serial form three essays of a projected five based
on his observations there, but he disagreed with the censorious
editor and withdrew the last two. The whole work was published posthumously in 1866. *A Yankee in Canada* is unworthy
of Thoreau. In it, he looks at what he regards as a backward
group of people, their alien and cramping religion, their use-
less soldiery, and pinched nature all about them. He jingo-
istically compares almost everything to its superior counter-
parts nearer Concord. He does tolerantly express artistic and
emotional appreciation of Notre Dame, the Catholic church
in Montreal, but he appears to do this mainly in order to add
that American churches have properly atrophied in happily
transcendental times. "In Concord, to be sure, we do not need
such. Our forests are such a church, far grander and more
sacred." Thoreau is generous enough to admit that he saw little
of Canada and would have liked to see some of its wilder
parts.

Journal, 1906, 1958. Shortly after Thoreau graduated from
Harvard in 1837, he began his lifelong habit of keeping a
journal, which twenty-four years later had come to about
2,000,000 words in thirty-nine manuscript notebooks. He built
a stout wooden box for them and at his death bequeathed the
priceless legacy to his sister Sophia. She left them to H. G. O.
Blake at her death; from 1881 to 1892, he inaccurately edited
sections of them, publishing *Early Spring in Massachusetts,*
1881; *Summer,* 1884; *Winter,* 1888; and *Autumn,* 1892. These

volumes helped to augment Thoreau's reputation but also to
suggest wrongly that his main interest in journal-keeping had
been scientific. In 1906 Bradford Torrey, who had transcribed
all the available journal material while it was in the possession
of Blake's legatee, and Francis H. Allen of Houghton Mifflin
Company published what was called Thoreau's complete journal in fourteen volumes. But in 1912 another volume appeared
for sale, and it was bought by the J. Pierpont Morgan Library
of New York, to go with the thirty-eight manuscript volumes
and Thoreau's wooden box, all of which the Morgan Library
had acquired three years before. Perry Miller edited this formerly lost journal, 1840-41, as *Consciousness in Concord,*
published in 1958 (Boston: Houghton Mifflin Company). Now
all of Thoreau's journal material has been published except
some writing which Thoreau himself used from his journal to
compile his *Maine Woods,* 1864, and except a 40,000-word
1846 notebook, which the New York Public Library now owns.
In almost every way Thoreau's journal is his most characteristic
work. Even *Walden,* which grew out of it and which is Thoreau's most eloquent public performance, is less typical of the
man than the infinitely varied and compelling journal. Here
we find the essential Thoreau—immediate, observant, witty,
philosophical, poetic, mystical, serene. *Walden* is a conscious
work of art, by comparison; the journal shows us, as though
we are looking over his shoulder, Thoreau in the act of
closely observing an elm or a pout or a tanager or a woodchuck, for example, or following the puzzling ramifications
of a certain thought, on, say, nature, wealth, science, poverty,
solitude, writing, or religion. Many entries are terse and fac-
tual and as such are useful mainly to the biographer. Others
are skillfully turned, informal essays, among the finest that
American literature affords. The devotee of *Walden* can turn
to Thoreau's journal and often find recorded there raw experi-

ences and initial thoughts on them which became carefully produced art in *Walden*. This journal ranks as high as any similar work produced by other American writers, for example, by Emerson, Hawthorne, Twain, or Henry James. Undoubtedly the best way to begin a study of this journal is to read *The Heart of Thoreau's Journals,* excellently selected and edited by Odell Shepard (Boston: Houghton Mifflin Company, 1927; rev. ed., New York: Dover Publications, Inc., 1961). The 1906, fourteen-volume journal was reprinted in full by Dover Publications, Inc., in two huge volumes in 1962.

THOREAU'S POETRY AND LETTERS

Many of Thoreau's poems were published in the *Dial*. Dozens of others first appeared in *A Week on the Concord and Merrimack Rivers,* and a few more in *Walden*. Thoreau evidently never attempted to gather them together for book publication. Long after his death, his friend F. B. Sanborn and Thoreau's English biographer H. S. Salt published a collection of his verse as *Poems of Nature,* 1895. In 1943 Carl Bode first published all of his verse in *Collected Poems of Henry Thoreau* (Chicago: Packard and Company). Thoreau regarded himself mainly as a poet in his early maturity, but gradually his prose became more poetic and his poetry was consequently neglected. Without much doubt Emerson's final judgment of Thoreau's poetry is correct: "His own verses are often rude and defective. The gold does not yet run pure, is drossy and crude. . . . his genius was better than his talent." Usually Thoreau seems more concerned with the soul of his poetry than with its body and drapery, that is, his prosody is often careless—his diction is old-fashioned, his rhymes are forced, his rhythm is jerky and prosaic, his imagery is not sustained, his development is truncated, and so on. At the same time, a dozen or so of his slightly more than two hundred poems are splendidly moving. Perhaps the best are "Within the Circuit of This Plodding Life," "Great God, I Ask Thee for No Meaner Pelf," "Light-Winged Smoke, Icarian Bird" (*Walden, XIII, 16*), "Low in the Eastern Sky," "Rumors from an Aeolian Harp," "Low-Anchored Cloud," "Woof of the Sun, Ethereal Gauze," "Lately, Alas, I Knew a Gentle Boy," "Let Such Pure Hate Still Underprop," "The Inward Morning," "I Am a Parcel of Vain Strivings Tied," "Fog," "Brother Where Dost Thou Dwell?", "I Am the Little Irish Boy," "The Virgin," "Whate'er We Leave to God, God Does," and "A Winter and Spring Scene." Thoreau is partly in the stream of metaphysical verse, stemming from British poets such as John Donne and George Herbert. This school was not popular in Thoreau's day, although Emerson and a little later Herman Melville and Emily Dickinson effectively used some seventeenth-century techniques in their poetry. But metaphysical poets have been popular in the twentieth century, much of the poetic taste of which has been conditioned by A. E. Housman, Gerard Manley Hopkins, William Butler Yeats, and T. S. Eliot. Therefore, his eclectic combination of the down-to-earth, the impressionistic, the symbolic, and the gnomic has made Thoreau the poet an imperfect forerunner of today. Nonetheless, as a final word on his poetry, it ought to be said that there are prose passages in *Walden* (for example, I, 16; IV, 2; V, 1, 16-17; XI, 11; XVIII, 11) which are more poetic than any "poem" Thoreau ever wrote.

Thoreau's letters, 1865, 1894, 1906, 1958. In 1865 Emerson published a small and biased selection of Thoreau's letters, called *Letters to Various Persons*. Its purpose was to reveal Thoreau as a perfect stoic. It succeeded, but less well than if Sophia Thoreau had not forced the publisher to include in the edition a few letters which also revealed her brother's natural affection. In 1894 F. B. Sanborn lovingly but unprofessionally edited *Familiar Letters of Henry David Thoreau.* In 1906 he released a slightly larger edition. Sanborn's work was twice as large as Emerson's but still nowhere near complete. After that a few more Thoreau letters were published here and there. But not until 1958 was any kind of justice done to Thoreau the letter-writer. In that year Walter Harding and Carl Bode, with admirable devotion and professional competence, published *The Correspondence of Henry David Thoreau* (New York: New York University Press). This collection contains every available letter by and also to Thoreau, and is in addition enriched by much historical and biographical information. The almost infinite number of facets of Thoreau's personality gleam in his letters. Thoreau was down to earth and practical in his shop talk with editors. He was frank and loyal in letters to members of his family. And he revealed his quirks, humanity, learning, stylistic lavishness, and fiery firmness of opinion to all those whom he respected enough to number among his correspondents.

To sum it all up, one might justly say that the reader of Thoreau's best works, especially his immortal *Walden,* soon learns to appreciate the man for three main reasons. In the first place, he is a challenging stylist, demanding the utmost intellectual and emotional alertness in the reader. In the second place, his life-long love of nature is so contagious that the responsive reader promises himself to do a little more hiking and camping and gardening, at least. And in the third place, he is such a forceful arguer of his position on simplicity, anti-materialism, individualism, politics, and many other aspects of life that the reader, hard put to defend his own prejudices, often abandons some of them and henceforth goes out a devotee of Henry David Thoreau.

FOR FURTHER READING

Books and articles about Thoreau are bewilderingly numerous. The following are suggested as being particularly illuminating:

Canby, Henry Seidel. *Thoreau*. Boston: Houghton Mifflin Company, 1939. A big, fact-crammed biography, charmingly written. It is somewhat weak, however, on Thoreau's Harvard years, is probably erroneous in contending that Thoreau was in love with Emerson's wife, and is in addition outmoded to some extent by more recent scholarship.

Christy, Arthur. *The Orient in American Transcendentalism: A Study of Emerson, Thoreau, and Alcott*. New York: Columbia University Press, 1932. The definitive study on the subject.

Derleth, August. *Concord Rebel: A Life of Henry D. Thoreau*. Philadelphia: Chilton Co., 1962. A reliable biography designed for younger readers.

Harding, Walter, ed. *Thoreau: A Century of Criticism*. Dallas: Southern Methodist University Press, 1954. Twenty-four major critical essays from Thoreau's time to ours.

Harding, Walter. *A Thoreau Handbook*. New York: New York University Press, 1959; paper, 1961. Chapters on Thoreau's life, works, sources, ideas, and fame, each chapter with a summary and an evaluation of pertinent scholarship.

Harding, Walter, ed. *Thoreau: Man of Concord*. New York: Holt, Rinehart and Winston, 1960. An anthology of more than a hundred sketches and reminiscences of Thoreau by his contemporaries.

Harding, Walter, ed. *The Variorum Walden by Henry D. Thoreau*. New York: Twayne Publishers, Inc., 1962. By far the finest edition of Thoreau's *Walden,* fully annotated and with unobtrusive, brief summaries of all pertinent scholarship.

Krutch, Joseph Wood. *Henry David Thoreau.* New York: William Sloane Associates, 1948. Probably the best-balanced biography; stresses Thoreau's ideas.

Lane, Lauriat, Jr., ed. *Approaches to Walden.* San Francisco: Wadsworth Publishing Company, Inc., 1961. A well-organized collection of about thirty essays, some by Thoreau's contemporaries and the rest modern, together with suggested questions and topics, and a bibliography.

Leary, Lewis. "Thoreau," pp. 153-206, in *Eight American Authors: A Review of Research and Criticism,* ed. by Floyd Stovall. New York: The Modern Language Association of America, 1956. With Bibliographical Supplement by J. Chesley Mathews. New York: W. W. Norton & Company, Inc., 1963. The best selective and descriptive bibliography. The serious reader should also consult the annual bibliographies of the *Publications of the Modern Language Association,* and the quarterly bibliographies of *American Literature,* for an indication of current scholarship on Thoreau.

Matthiessen, F. O. *The American Renaissance: Art and Expression in the Age of Emerson and Whitman.* New York: Oxford University Press, 1941. Analyzes Thoreau's life and works, and sets both in the context of the careers of Emerson, Hawthorne, Melville, and Whitman.

Paul, Sherman, ed. *Thoreau: A Collection of Critical Essays.* Englewood Cliffs, N.J.: Prentice-Hall, Inc., 1962. Fifteen essays by perceptive modern critics.

Seybold, Ethel. *Thoreau: The Quest and the Classics.* New Haven: Yale University Press, 1951. Analyzes the influence of classical literature on Thoreau's intellectual and literary development.

Shanley, J. Lyndon. *The Making of Walden, with the Text of the First Version*. Chicago: University of Chicago Press, 1957. A careful study of the drafts of *Walden* and an analysis of their changes and growth.

Sherwin, J. Stephen, and Richard C. Reynolds. *A Word Index to Walden with Textual Notes*. Charlottesville: University of Virginia Press, 1960. A concordance of *Walden;* invaluable for those who wish to study Thoreau's diction, imagery, and related matters, and for those who may wish to locate an imperfectly remembered quotation from *Walden*.

Stoller, Leo. *After Walden: Thoreau's Changing Views on Economic Man*. Stanford: Stanford University Press, 1957. A study of the changes in Thoreau's attitudes toward social and economic man in the fifteen years after Thoreau left Walden Pond.

NOTES

NOTES

NOTES

NOTES

NOTES

NOTES

NOTES

NOTES

NOTES

NOTES

NOTES

NOTES

NOTES

NOTES